Lessons in Leadership

50 ways to avoid falling into the 'Trump' Trap

By Ann Andrews CSP

MOREAU
publishing
building brand authority through authorship

Published By Moreau Publishing

Email   info@moreaupublishing.com

Website   www.moreaupublishing.com

A catalog record for this book is available from the
National Library of New Zealand.

ISBN - 978-0-9876590-9-5

First published 2017 by Moreau Publishing

Cover design by Don Henderson

POD Edition

Dedication

To my amazing grandparents
Frances Edward Stuart (1901-1967)
Mildred Stuart (1904-1982)

My grandparents raised me until I was 6 years old.

My grandmother had to leave school at 12 years of age when her mother died. She had no choice but to take on the responsibility of looking after her father and three younger sisters. At 12 years old. She lived through two world wars and a depression and raised her own three children during times of great turmoil; hardship and deprivation.

No-one ever went hungry or cold on her watch. She was of the generation that wasted nothing. Food was never, ever thrown out. She survived two bouts of cancer in days when people were not expected to survive cancer. I never heard her complain about her lot. She just got on with things.

I've often wondered how different her life could have been if she had been able to finish school and not have to shoulder so much responsibility at such an incredibly young age.

My grandfather was a stonemason. He enlisted and fought in the 1st World War when he was too young to enlist; he enlisted and fought in the 2nd World War when he was actually too old to enlist.

In the 2nd World War, he was wounded and for the rest of his life walked with a serious and painful limp. We can only assume that it was in that same war that he lost a lung but we will never know because our family didn't find out that he only had one lung until after his death. He kept that information totally to himself.

Although they were never even remotely rich, they were humble, hard working, honest and respectful.

My grandfather hated bullies and was known to take on men much bigger, younger and stronger than himself. If he felt apprentice builders or young workers male and female were being unfairly treated he never hesitated to step in to protect them. He wasn't a large man yet he stood up men much tougher and stronger than him using only his calm grace and dignity.

He was a quiet leader who went about his work without fear or favor. Both grandparents lived their beliefs and values every day of their lives. Their values became my values.

This book is dedicated to them because they were my base camp. They were everything I aspired to be.

Acknowledgements

Over the 30+ years, I've been working in the Human Resources sector, I've met many, many amazing leaders. Not all of them the CEO's or General Managers of the various organizations I've consulted with. Many of them were ordinary people on shop floors or front offices who displayed every aspect of leadership this book promotes, my thanks go to them.

Huge thanks to my poor husband went through months of my Trump dark days. He deserves every ounce of credit for supporting me through my very vocal shock, horror, and disbelief as Donald Trump became President of the USA. He probably kept me alive by reminding me every day, to keep taking my blood pressure pills.

Once I'd decided to turn my horror into affirmative action Eugene Moreau (an American) supported me every step of the way in the decision to convert my angst into a book. Don Henderson was the amazing editor who toned down my emotions and crafted them into positive lessons for future leaders.

It was imperative to me to show young people arriving in our workplaces and moving into various leadership roles that the Trump way of leading is absolutely not one they would want to emulate.

A particular thank you goes to Rod Oram; journalist and speaker at one of my Big Thinking Business Forums earlier this year, for permission to use his musings on the damage he felt Trump was about to inflict.

About Ann Andrews CSP

Ann Andrews has spent over 30 years working in the Human Resources arena. Not only a recognized specialist in change management and building high performing teams, she is passionate about the need for organizations to learn, unlearn and relearn, to understand the power and responsibilities of 'leadership'.

She was the creator of 'The Corporate Toolbox' an online community for business owners and is the current CEO of 'Big Thinking Business' through which she holds regular forums for business owners who want to take their organizations to the next level of growth.

Ann is an avid writer and blogger, she is the author of several books and numerous eBooks covering all aspects of human behavior. She is determined to show anyone who is in a management position, that the aggressive leadership behaviors we are currently witnessing in several countries, are not the behaviors we want them to emulate.

Dame Anita Roddick – founder of The Body Shop once famously said 'if you think one person can't make a difference, try going to bed with a mosquito'. The choice countries and organizations need to make is do they want their leaders to make a difference for the better or the worse.

What People Say

'Ann Andrews has condensed decades of leadership wisdom in a treasure trove of simple, useable insights...

These ideas have a timeless quality which will be useful for young and old alike.

"The leadership lessons from Donald Trump" arrives at an important time, where technology and disruption challenge the human experience on a daily basis. And we are confused by what we see in the media which often is disconnected from our own reality..

This book provides useable punchy and memorable how-to's to lift our spirit and motivate the reader to want to be a better leader.'"

Kim Campbell
CEO Employers' and Manufacturers Association

'As a speaker and adviser committed to evolutionary commerce and the essential disruption that embraces, I absolutely love this book. Learning and living leadership is vital for anyone who wants a better world. Ann does, and in these wonderful words, she goes beautifully about helping us create it. I'm particularly charmed that a potentially negative and critical set of observations has been re-framed to give us superbly helpful guidelines with which to go forward. Thank you Ann!'

Catherine Palin-Brinkworth M.AppSci (Social Ecology)
Behavioural Scientist - Business Growth Strategist -
Leadership Mentor, Speaker and Facilitator

'At a time when public confidence in leadership is at an all-time low, Ann's book is as relevant as it is timely.

Beautifully capturing the Zeitgeist of American politics today, 50 Lessons in Leadership is the ideal read for anyone looking to avoid the pitfalls of 'presidency', to restore trust and to contribute to a better world.'

Simon Tupman
Author, 'Why Entrepreneurs Should Eat Bananas'

'I first came across Ann over 25 years ago when I needed someone to run a workshop with a group of pharmacy owners who thought they knew everything they needed to know about change management and leadership. Some hours later, and after some subtle poking in the chest by Ann, they found out they didn't! I was fortunate to connect with her again recently when we were both guest speaking at a business seminar; and nothing has changed. She is a thought provoker, provocative and passionate about business and how leadership is a defining component when it comes to being successful, or not, and her latest book Lessons in Leadership: How to avoid falling into the Trump trap is absolutely a book for our times..'

Paul Gianotti
Executive General Manager - Warehouse Stationery

Contents

Introduction

50 ways to avoid falling into the 'Trump' trap

I watched the US presidential election in absolute shock and dismay. I saw behaviors that left me speechless and a drop in any resemblance of professional standards as Donald Trump stepped over, trampled on, abused and generally ridiculed every person he debated with on the campaign trail and even some poor unfortunates in his audiences.

By the time the Hillary/Donald debates took place, it was clear that vital issues were not important to Trump. It was more about humiliating his opponent with all manner of insults and innuendo. The entire election process was an abysmal lesson in leadership for our children and grandchildren, particularly when you consider that this was effectively the recruitment process for one of the most critical leadership positions in the world.

The day that Donald Trump was confirmed as the new President of the USA, I simply could not believe my eyes or ears and I was left feeling physically sick.

Why was I even interested? I live in New Zealand, so what did it matter who took on that office?

It mattered to me because for the past 30 years I've worked in the Human Resources arena and 'leadership' in my book, is everything. If a team isn't working – look at the leader. If a business is failing – look at the leader. If a country is falling apart and/or bankrupt – look at the leader.

Since the end of World War II America had been one of the 'gold standards' of democratic leadership across the globe. That didn't mean that America was perfect. I think the gloss wore off considerably under 'Dubya' (George W Bush Junior) and his questionable invasion of Iraq.

Allegedly the Bush administration were looking for those elusive 'weapons of mass destruction' which pretty much everyone else in the Western world suspected were not there. Undaunted, Bush instigated the invasion of Iraq. Was the invasion a genuine desire to free the country from a tyrant or a smoke-screen to capture the country's oil? After all, Bush was an oil man.

Still, I had a belief that America would see through all the Trump 'bluff' and do the right thing; that people would be sickened by his ranting and rhetoric and NOT vote for him. I'd always been so impressed with President Obama's calm grace and dignity – the exact opposite of Donald in every way it seemed.

Obama represented America's unshakeable belief that no matter your color or creed or even the circumstances of your birth, anything was possible.

Despite being vicious on the election trail to anyone who opposed him. Despite all the personal scandals that surfaced during the election trail. Despite the endless 'fake,' 'alternative' and prefabricated truths. Despite Hillary beating him hands down in every debate. Despite refusing to release his tax returns and despite losing the 'popular vote' by 3 million – he won the election.

During the campaign, I kept waiting and waiting for people to challenge him for the appalling things he said and the shocking things he did. It was as if we had entered an alternative universe where every day he would do or say something that left me aghast and I would wonder why people were not speaking up. Why his fellow Republicans were not challenging him or better still, why they were not finding a way to remove him from the election trail.

And then the worst nightmare happened – he became POTUS. How?

Because deliberately and skillfully he tapped into fear and discontent.

The middle classes or 'rust belt' had been promised the 'dream' and in reality had been seriously left behind because of advances in technology. And their discontent was very real. These were the people who a generation ago would have been the backbone of America. The ordinary, hard working people who had built the car industry, the steel industry, the coal, and oil sector.

But the world had moved on.

Other countries were now able to manufacture all of these commodities for a fraction of the price. There was now empirical data proving that oil and coal were huge contributors to climate change and most forward thinking businesses and countries were rapidly moving to clean energy sources. So those middle-income jobs vanished, and these hard working people were left feeling distinctly disenfranchised.

Shame on preceding governments who had done nothing to alert people to the fact that technological change was a reality and their jobs were at risk.

It wasn't just Americans that were facing the challenge - the whole world was literally in the same boat. Yet if any of the leaders of any of those sectors had been forward thinking, they could have set up training programs to up-skill these people. If any of these communities had had good leaders, they could have been looking for other businesses to come into their communities – they could have created new jobs.

They could have shown leadership. Sadly they didn't.

So people found themselves unemployed, watching helplessly as their once vibrant communities died and as a result, they became increasingly poor, sidelined and angry.

And then along came Donald Trump promising to take away their pain, to bring their jobs back. He promised he would return things to how they used to be so their pride and ability to provide for their families would be restored. He promised that any American company that shipped jobs overseas would be harshly penalized. He promised to put tariffs on any commodities that were coming in from outside America. He promised to make America great again. He let these people believe in the dream again, even though he never could turn back the clock.

This book then is a result of my personal frustration of watching such a man sell his daily lies to ordinary people.

I believe the American voters have been sold a bill of goods. That they've fallen under the spell of a snake oil salesman. The American people are worth more and they deserve better. The tragedy is that at some stage of Trump's presidency, people will wake up and realize they have been duped. Unfortunately for now, it is too late.

This book is my way of saying that the behaviors Trump displays are NOT leadership behaviors.

In the words of Thomas Jefferson, "All tyranny requires to gain a foothold is for people of good conscience to remain silent," and I simply cannot remain silent.

So here are my 50 Lessons in leadership, literally taken from the first 236 days of watching Trump churn out the worst version of leadership I've witnessed in my lifetime.

Although these lessons are intended for leaders in the business world, they apply equally to any leadership role. Those leaders within the business sphere realm need only substitute the words 'owner or manager' for the words 'politician or political party' to make the lessons relevant.

How This Book Is Written

This book would not have made sense if it was just a collection of my own thoughts and opinions.

I can imagine anyone reading it asking 'who is this person and what does she know about America and American politics?'

These, of course, would be valid questions.

I am at an age where I have seen a fair few American presidents come and go; a fair few UK/European Prime Ministers come and go, and now that I live in New Zealand I've seen a brand new political system emerge rather than the two party system – for better or worse.

I've always been interested in politics, and have absolutely always been fascinated by leadership.

Having worked in the Human Resources field for over 30 years, I have had the good fortune to work with owners and managers in organizations of all shapes and sizes. Moreover, I have worked with and witnessed amazing leaders over the years, alongside some abysmal ones.

So as I became annoyed; angry; confused and even downright incredulous as each bizarre Trump day passed, I started reading everything I could from a variety of reputable news sources around the Western world to check that I wasn't alone in feeling the way I did. And by doing this, I decided on the following format so that you the reader could see I wasn't alone in my fears and my views.

Throughout the chapters, you will see:

1. A 'headline' from some aspect of the Trump presidency from a reliable news source.

2. An 'extract' from that article.

3. A 'lesson' current and potential leaders could use to learn from the behaviors outlined in the article.

I begin this journey into understanding Donald Trump with the question 'What IS Leadership?' I then continue with a variety of chapters which will include what I think are the lessons we can all learn from him.

Chapter 1: I cover the need for all of us to know our limits. To know when we are taking on more than we can realistically cope with, for whatever reason.

Chapter 2: I talk about understanding our communication styles and methods. For sure Donald has immortalized 'tweets' for better or worse.

Chapter 3: I recommend the need for a new managers/leaders/politicians to create a few successes early on in their term; not only to give themselves confidence but also to comfort the people who put them into the role. No-one wants to admit they have backed a loser.

Chapter 4: I discuss the need to build on what has gone before us rather than trying to destroy everything our predecessor/s implemented.

Chapter 5: I caution managers and leaders to be alert to warning signs that all is not well in their sphere. To be aware that their ideas may not be working as well as they had hoped; to face facts that early results suggest they may either be going off track or worse – that they are now heading in the wrong direction altogether.

Chapter 6: I alert managers and leaders to understanding conflicts of interest and the dangers to their reputation if their followers perceive that what they are doing doesn't quite pass the 'smell test' as one pundit called it.

Chapter 7: I move to talking about the people a leader recruits into his or her team and the impression that gives. I discuss the need to understand not only their own skill set but the skill set of the closest advisors and team members; in particular the need to be aware of the skills gaps if they want to lead a fully functioning organization.

Chapter 8: I wanted to cover the fact that all of us at some stage of our lives need to seek advice; to listen to wise counsel. Leaders need to be particularly aware of not falling into the trap of surrounding themselves with 'yes' people. Seeking advice from a variety of sources isn't a weakness it is actually a strength – it says we acknowledge that we don't know everything and that we can listen to different opinions.

Chapter 9: This chapter concentrates on a leader understanding the need and the courage required to build a future versus trying to resurrect an outdated past.

Chapter 10: Asks anyone in a leadership role to consider the legacy they want to leave; to think about how they want to be remembered. We may be living and working in the 'now', but people have long memories.

Chapter 11: I discuss the enormous challenges that come with being in any leadership role. I look at how the Democratic Party failed their base. I ponder whether Donald wanted to be a dictator or a martyr and I explore the roller coaster of events he has mis-handled which could cause his demise.

Chapter 12: I look at life after Trump and the challenges of global leadership in an ever changing and increasingly dangerous world. I summarize what I believe is the good news that has arisen out of a Trump presidency; the really good news; the not so great news and the exceptionally good news.

Prologue

Defining Leadership

"Before you are a leader, success is all about growing yourself. When you become a leader, success is all about growing others."

Jack Welch

Before we enter into any discussion about leadership, especially bad leadership, we must first at the very least provide some parameter of thought or context to defining what good leadership is. The characteristics and traits of a good leader are many due to the diverse nature of the leadership role, their personal leadership style and even the operational environment in which they find themselves.

All leaders are different. There's a myriad of different personality types and there is no one size fits all. Look at the different personalities of say, Warren Buffet and Sir Richard Branson, two incredibly successful leaders but two vastly different personalities.

However, I've always believed that there are four very simple principles of leadership, which, if followed can form a solid base upon which to build.

1. Know yourself warts and all. Know your strengths and your weaknesses. Acknowledge them; don't try to hide them. Recruit people who compliment those skills and you will have a balanced team and a great decision making process.

2. Have a Vision that inspires. People will line up to join an organization with a great Vision. Remember John F Kennedy's 'man on the moon by the end of the decade'... how inspiring was that?

3. Instil an ethical set of values. Your people need to know what is important when they too make decisions. If you decide that 'customer service' is your highest value, then your people will look after your customers. If you decide that 'quality' is your highest value then once again they will know what is important. We must also ensure that those values are ethical. The very worst thing we can do to our followers is put them in a position which makes them vulnerable. Know the difference between right and wrong so they will know also.

4. Surround yourself with great people and look after them. A leader is nothing without followers.

In an article written by Jennifer Post and posted on the Business News Daily website, eleven leaders were asked to define what leadership means to them, and from which the following eleven traits emerged:

1. **The pursuit of bettering your environment.**
   "There is no one-size-fits-all approach, answer key or formula to leadership. Leadership should be the humble, authentic expression of your unique personality in pursuit of bettering whatever environment you are in."
   Katie Christy, founder, Activate Your Talent

2. **Knowing your team and yourself well.**
   "To me, leadership is about playing to strengths and addressing weaknesses in the most productive and efficient way possible. It's about knowing your team and yourself, and doing your best job to set both up for success."
   Samantha Cohen, co-founder, Neon Bandits

3. **Giving people the tools to succeed.**
   "Leadership is serving the people that work for you by giving them the tools they need to succeed. Your workers should be looking forward to the customer and not backwards, over their shoulders, at you. It also means genuine praise for what goes well and leading by taking responsibility early and immediately if things go bad."
   Jordan French, founding CMO, BeeHex, Inc. 3D Food Printing

4. **Open, authentic and positive influence.**
   "Leadership comes from influence, and influence can come from anyone at any level and in any role. Being open and authentic, helping to lift others up and working toward a common mission, build influence. True leadership comes when those around you are influenced by your life in a positive way."
   Kurt Uhlir, CEO and co-founder Sideqik

5. **Clarity, confidence, and courage.**
"A leader is someone who has the clarity to know the right things to do, the confidence to know when she's wrong, and the courage to do the right things even when they're hard."

Darcy Eikenberg, founder, RedCapeRevolution.com

6. **Building consensus and common goals.**
"Leadership styles differ, but at the core, good leaders make the people they are leading accomplish more than they otherwise would. The most effective leaders do this not through fear, intimidation or title, but rather by building consensus around a common goal."

Tom Madine, CEO and president, Worldwide Express

7. **Being the solution to problems.**
"Leadership is the ability to see a problem and be the solution. So many people are willing to talk about problems or can even empathize, but not many can see the problem or challenge and rise to it. It takes a leader to truly see a problem as a challenge and want to drive toward it."

Andrea Walker-Leidy, owner, Walker Publicity Consulting

8. **Helping others achieve the impossible.**
"Leadership is the ability to help people achieve things they don't think are possible. Leaders are coaches with a passion for developing people, not players; they get satisfaction from achieving objects through others. Leaders inspire people through a shared vision and create an environment where people feel valued and fulfilled."

Randy Stocklin, co-founder and CEO, One Click Ventures

9. **Building the next generation of leaders.**
"A leader is someone who builds their team, mentors them and then advocates for them. A leader develops the talent around them to be more successful than he or she is — or to borrow from a mentor of mine, 'a leader trains his or her assassins.'"

J. Kelly Hoey, author, "Build Your Dream Network"

10. **Building followership.**
"Being a leader means building followership. Your primary responsibility is how you can inspire those around you to support a larger agenda under your direction and vision. You have to prioritize communications and [the] development of others. Your job is no longer about what you can accomplish, but what your entire team can achieve. Good leaders focus on 'we' not 'me.'"

Kristi Hedges, leadership coach and author, "The Inspiration Code"

11. Actively listening.

"In my experience, leadership is about three things: to listen, to inspire and to empower. Over the years, I've tried to learn to do a much better job of listening actively — making sure I really understand the other person's point of view, learning from them, and using that basis of trust and collaboration to inspire and empower."

Larry Garfield, president, Garfield Group Additional reporting by
Brittney Morgan

(Post. Business News Daily. 2017)

Chapter 1

Know yourself – warts and all

"Man is not what he thinks he is,
he is what he hides."

André Malraux

Lesson 1: Be 100% aware of your behaviors during a recruitment/election process.

The second debate, Donald Trump and Hillary Clinton spar in bitter, personal terms

'The initial exchange of fire in the wake of the release of Mr. Trump's crudely offensive remarks captured on videotape on Friday, followed by a moment in which Mr. Trump apparently threatened to try to put Mrs. Clinton in jail if he is elected (a threat that, as some have commented, looks like something close to an unprecedented authoritarian turn in American politics) were as electrifying as anything in a presidential debate.' (MARTINOCT, 2016)

These debates were the recruitment process for the President of the Unites States of America and Donald Trump really did not equip himself well (in my humble opinion). I've been on both sides of the recruitment process and I know firsthand that the interviewing and selection processes are stressful for both parties. But it is a process where, under tough questioning, an interviewer can decide on the suitability of a candidate. After all, no-one wants to recruit the wrong person!

If during the interview process there are signs that a candidate is erratic and disorganized - be alert.

If they don't answer direct questions or bad-mouth previous employers – be aware.

If they become agitated when you ask the 'tricky' questions and use various distracting techniques (changing the subject matter, making threatening comments or becoming defensive), then don't employ them and under no circumstances give them the nuclear codes.

"When people show you who they are, believe them."
Bianca Frazier

Lesson 2: Know when you have reached the top of your game.

Out of his depth Trump clings to deception

'During the debate, the points scored against Trump were damaging. But the points he ceded would disqualify any normal politician, in any normal presidential year. Trump drove a high-speed train filled with fireworks into a nuclear power plant. He was self-absorbed, prickly, defensive, interrupting, baited by every charge yet unprepared to refute them. During his share of a 90-minute debate, he was horribly out of his depth, incapable of stringing together a coherent three-sentence case. The postmodern quality of Trump's appeal culminated in an unbalanced rant claiming, "I also have a much better temperament than she has" — an assertion greeted by audience laughter. And Trump concluded his performance by praising himself for his own grace and restraint, during an evening that showed him to be nasty, witless and deceptive.

His behaviors and personality were clearly on display during the campaign, yet still, people listened to the words he said rather than the behavior they witnessed. It should now be clear to Republicans: Vanity is his strategy.' (GERSON. 2016)

◆◆◆◆◆◆◆

'A Trump Biographer says that 'He was of the school of thought that there was no such thing as bad publicity. He was also of the school that if anyone says anything bad, you sue them. A very litigious guy' (Clibbon, 2016). And with regard to Trump running for office, she suggests "They voted for a guy who could fix it, the CEO, on The Apprentice for 10 years, who could make a deal with anybody. The tactics that served Trump so well in business – playing the alpha male, holding one-on-one meetings – did not translate to politics. Now he's up against 535 other people [in the House and Senate], other people who have their own independent power base and are not really interested in rolling over. The model of taking one person in a room and beating up on them doesn't work with 535.' (BLAIR, Quotes)

Howard Fineman asks 'Why does a man who claims such great success as a business manager seem so overwhelmed?' He goes on to say 'Democrats have taken their time filling his Cabinet, arguing, with much justification, that Trump had presented them with a roster of conflict-laden billionaires and ideologues antagonistic to the goals of the departments they had been nominated to lead. But there a host of in-house reasons for the first month's mess'. Here they are:

He only wants to talk to people who have no choice but to agree with him, or who are glad to tell him why his enemies are scum.

As leaders, we all have to learn that what serves us in one job may not serve us in another. Part of a career path is absolutely to find something that stretches us, but not one that is light years away from our skills and one that we are clearly unsuited for.

Which leads us to understand the Peter Principle.

'The Peter Principle is based on the logical idea that competent employees will continue to be promoted, but at some point will be promoted into positions for which they are incompetent, and they will then remain in those positions because of the fact that they do not demonstrate any further competence that would get them recognized for additional promotion. According to the Peter Principle, every position in a given hierarchy will eventually be filled by employees who are incompetent to fulfill the job duties of their respective positions.' (INVESTOPEDIA)

As a businessman, Trump controls his own companies, hiring and firing his own people, and answering to no-one except, perhaps, shareholders and banks. What made him think he could work that way as POTUS?

Did he really think things through? Was it that he wanted more power? Did he want to be a hero? Was it that he was bored with just making money? (Though we never did get to see those tax returns.) So perhaps he wasn't quite as good at making money as he would have us believe. Or was it that he saw the potential for making even more money if he became the President of the USA?

Who knows?

All I know is that when I first heard he was running for POTUS, like the rest of the world, I thought it was a joke. Then the laugh was on us when he did it. Now I think the laugh is on him because he is so clearly out of his depth it is embarrassing and terrifying. I just hope someone has those nuclear codes hidden away from him.

So I suggest, that the most vital strength of any leader then, is to know themselves inside and out, warts and all, and in particular to know their limits.

This isn't an easy realization for any of us to accept. But moving into a role you are clearly unsuited for or which is way beyond your talents and capabilities, is actually a recipe for a nervous breakdown or in his case possible impeachment.

"The Donald is not a master of the deal; he is a reckless, foolhardy craps dealer playing with house money. He doesn't care at all about the lives and fortunes of the human beings peopling this planet."

(Gizmo, 2016)

Lesson 3: Be very careful whom you offend on the way up the corporate ladder; for surely you will meet them again on your way down.

On Trump's second day thousands of women march.

'Trump has angered many liberal Americans with comments seen as demeaning to women, Mexicans and Muslims, and worried some abroad with his inaugural vow on Friday to put "America First" in his decision making.' (MALONE, 2017)

In the case of Donald, it is probably easier to find someone he 'hasn't' offended than those he has. He has offended women, the disabled, John McCain – a decorated war hero; the mother of the Muslim American soldier who was killed fighting for America, and even Angela Merkle. Then, of course, there's everyone who stood against him during the election campaign, plus Mexicans, people of color and transgender; the list goes on.

He offended Sens. Ted Cruz of Texas and Marco Rubio of Florida who paid him back by recently voting against Trump's repeal of Obamacare. Didn't Trump call Ted a [i]'pussy' and nick-named Marco Rubio [ii]'little Marco'.

Oh dear.

On day 161 of his presidency he offended 'bigly' when he posted this tweet:

Donald J. Trump ✔
@realDonaldTrump — Follow

I heard poorly rated @Morning_Joe speaks badly of me (don't watch anymore). Then how come low I.Q. Crazy Mika, along with Psycho Joe, came..

5:52 AM - 29 Jun 2017

President Trump angrily lashes out at 'Morning Joe' hosts on Twitter

"President Trump lashed out at the hosts of MSNBC's "Morning Joe" in two vicious tweets Thursday morning, calling Mika Brzezinski "low I.Q. Crazy Mika" and claiming she had a facelift late last year." (JOHNSON, 2017)

Is this really how we want a country leader to behave?

We teach our children not to call people 'names' and yet here is the supposed leader of the free World name calling like someone in the 1st grade.

People will retaliate. Perhaps not immediately, sometimes it may take a while for our followers to realize they've been insulted, put down or minimized in some way because most of us wouldn't dream of doing that to someone else.

Insults cost a leader. The fight-back from people you have ridiculed, trashed or generally degraded will happen. In Trump's case, the fight-back began on just his second day in office.

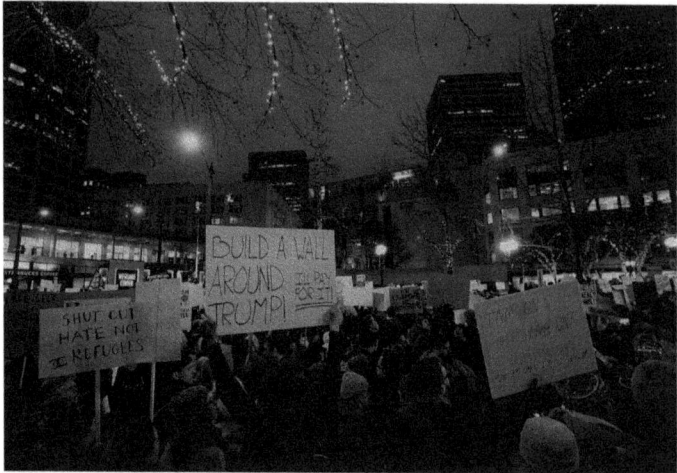

"Karma comes after everyone eventually. You can't get away with screwing people over your whole life, I don't care who you are. What goes around comes around. That's how it works. Sooner or later the universe will serve you the revenge that you deserve."

Jessica Brody

[i] Daily News - Donald Trump criticizes Ted Cruz, calls him a 'pussy' at New Hampshire rally. http://www.nydailynews.com/news/politics/donald-trump-calls-ted-cruz-pussy-n-h-rally-article-1.2524951
[ii] Daily Mail - 'Get in the plane and go home. It's over there': Trump is caught cold-shouldering his newest endorser Chris Christie on hot mic as he tears into 'little Marco' Rubio. http://www.dailymail.co.uk/news/article-3467674/Trump-blasts-little-Marco-Rubio-not-causing-stir-cold-shouldering-endorser-Chris-Christie-plane-home-s-home.html

Lesson 4: Be careful who you brand the enemy and resist playing tit-for-tat.

Trump launches all-out attack on the press

'Trump has repeatedly called out individual reporters on Twitter and in interviews for everything from what he viewed as insufficient crowd camera shots to biased reporting. And attacking the press is a regular part of the presumptive Republican nominee's stump speech, during which he typically rips reporters as "scum," "slime," "dishonest" and "disgusting" — often prompting jeers from the crowd.'

The blog continues: 'The news conference came four months after Trump claimed to have raised $6 million for veterans groups, but then dodged reporters' questions about which groups had received the donations. Trump kicked off his litany of media attacks Tuesday by accusing reporters of cynically turning what should have been a positive story about his charitable work into a negative one. Reporters had for months repeatedly asked Trump to provide an accounting of the donations, requests that were frequently rebuffed or side-stepped by Trump and his campaign staff.' (DIAMOND, 2016)

And so as payback to the journalists Trump refused to attend the annual [iii]Correspondents Dinner. He will be the first President since Ronald Reagan not to attend, and the reason Reagan didn't attend was that he was recovering from injuries he sustained in an assassination attempt. Trump's comments: [iv]"Let there be no more 'sources' cited in news stories, because fake news media just make them up when they have none". He called on media to stop making up stories based on nonexistent confidential "sources".

♦♦♦♦♦♦♦

Trump bans American journalists, but not Russian press, from meeting with Russian foreign minister

"The only public event on President Trump's calendar the day after he fired FBI Director James Comey amid an ongoing investigation into his campaign's ties with Russian officials was a White House meeting with Russian Foreign Minister Sergey Lavrov. American media was banned from covering the event. A Russian photographer, however, was not, so the American public was able to see images of the meeting thanks to Russia's state-run press.." (RUPAR, 2017)

♦♦♦♦♦♦♦

Trump team keeps U.S. reporters in the dark overseas

"President Donald Trump has left American journalists in the dark during key moments of his nine-day foreign trip, delaying readouts, keeping reporters at a distance and not holding news conferences — which has allowed him to avoid having to answer to controversies at home.

The moves have continued a pattern established over the first months of his administration." (PALMERI, 2017)

◆◆◆◆◆◆◆

Reporter Who Called Out Sarah Huckabee Sanders: 'I Can't Take It Anymore'

"We are bullied and browbeaten every day — and I've pretty much had enough of it." "For the government to sit there and undermine, essentially what is very essential checks and balances system — it's disheartening," Karem said on MSNBC's "Morning Joe" Wednesday. "It's unnerving. I can't take it anymore. It's nuts."

◆◆◆◆◆◆◆

Tillerson blows up at top White House aide

"The secretary of state, frustrated by negative press coverage and delays in appointing staff, unleashed his anger in front of Reince Priebus, Jared Kushner and others. Secretary of State Rex Tillerson's frustrations with the White House have been building for months. Last Friday, they exploded. The normally laconic Texan unloaded on Johnny DeStefano, the head of the presidential personnel office, for torpedoing proposed nominees to senior State Department posts and for questioning his judgment." (DAWSON et al, 2017)

This behavior links back to Lesson 3. 'Be very careful whom you offend on the way up the corporate ladder - for surely you will meet them again on your way down', and even Lesson 12. 'As a leader, you must be able to deal with the 'tough' questions'.

Leaders need exposure as a way of marketing themselves, their products or services and in this case, their policies. Presidents need the press to be on their side. For sure, some reporters are simply out for headlines but a smart leader will ignore those. A smart leader would rise above the comments and sensationalism to show themselves as being bigger than that.

It's not a rocket science then to suggest the worst people to turn into enemies would be the press. And really – isn't Trump the biggest 'maker-upper' of stuff in the history of humanity?

However, I think the biggest lesson here is 'don't be vengeful', that is such a bad look. Getting back at people is such a waste of time and energy and in the end, only hurts you.

'Vengeance is the act of turning anger in on yourself.
On the surface, it may be directed at someone else,
but it's a sure-fire recipe for arresting emotional recovery.'

Jane Goldman

[iii] Independent - Donald Trump refuses to attend White House Correspondents' Association Dinner. http://www.independent.co.uk/news/world/americas/us-politics/donald-trump-white-house-correspondents-association-dinner-not-attending-twitter-a7599896.html
[iv] Thenet24h.com - Interview with President Donald Trump (Video). http://ca.thenet24h.com/283111/when-they-make-stories-when-they-create-sourcesi-believe-lot-stories-are-pure-ficti.html

Chapter 2

Understand your communication style and methods and how they affect others

'Better to Remain Silent and Be Thought a Fool
than to Speak and Remove All Doubt'

Mark Twain

Lesson 5: Don't use Twitter as your chief communication tool

Trump tweets that he won the 3rd debate

'If nothing else this election has taught us that if it's 3 a.m. somewhere there's a good chance Donald Trump is tweeting, and likely self-congratulating too — and so it proved Thursday morning after the Republican candidate landed in Ohio fresh from the final televised presidential debate in Las Vegas.

The tweet: "Thank you America — I am honored to win the final debate for our MOVEMENT. It is time to #DrainTheSwamp & #MAGA!" Trump said in a post published at 3:14 a.m. ET.

Still, according to a CNN/ORC poll of people who watched the debate, it was Democratic candidate Hillary Clinton who beat out Trump in their third debate, by a 13-point margin (Clinton 52%; Trump 39%) — although calling these debates can be more an art than science. That poll nevertheless gave Clinton a "clean sweep" of all three debates.' (HJELMGAARD. 2016)

◆◆◆◆◆◆◆

Trump tells German reporter he 'very seldom' regrets his tweets – and admits he uses Twitter to 'get around the media'

'President Donald Trump 'very seldom' regrets the tweets he sends out to his 27 million followers, the president revealed at a press conference Friday. Approaching two months in office where he has repeatedly jolted convention and upended the news with his online missives – often flitted out in the early hours of the morning – the president got asked about his Twitter habits while standing beside the staid German Chancellor Angela Merkel. And by the way, my second question, are there from time to time tweets that you regret in hindsight?' asked the reporter from Germany's Die Welt. 'Very seldom,' Trump responded.' (EARLE, 2017).

However, this is the tweet that set off a special investigation and which could end in disaster for Trump:

Donald J. Trump ✔
@realDonaldTrump

Follow

James Comey better hope that there are no "tapes" of our conversations before he starts leaking to the press!

5:26 AM - 12 May 2017

♦♦♦♦♦♦♦

President Trump tweets warning to fired FBI director Comey

'Now the top Democrat on the House intelligence committee is asking the president to hand over to Congress any recordings that might exist of his conversations with Comey. But California Rep. Adam Schiff says if recordings exist, it would be because President Donald Trump made them.' (WDRB. 13/5/2017)

Trump's need to tweet despite all the people around him telling him tweeting is a really bad idea says so many things about him. Why does he keep doing it?

Is it that:

- He doesn't sleep well because of all the chaos and that waking in the 'early hours' he finds tweeting a way to vent his anger/fear/frustration?

- He refuses to take advice from anyone because HE knows best? Who would be his lawyer?

- He knows deep down that he isn't doing well but that by sending tweets out to his base it gives him a boost in confidence and keeps them loyal?

- It is his way of obscuring and obfuscating whatever the issue of the day is – usually an issue he has created in the first place?

He can't live without drama?

Tragically what he is doing by tweeting is leaving an easily followed electronic trail so that when he later denies he said something, his tweets can be checked to prove that he actually did say that.

If you are worried as a leader; or feeling stressed or feeling uncertain or even unloved, write something in a journal – that is not only safer than sending tweets out to however million followers you have – but while you are writing it may even give you an insight as to what your fears and concerns are and what to do about them. And the bonus is that no-one gets to see what you have written; you can reflect at leisure safe in the knowledge that no-one knows that you are having a crisis of self-belief.

Leaders must have insight into how they affect their followers. But also, how they themselves can be instrumental in laying the ground work for their own demise.

"I think.... you still have no idea. The effect you can have."

Lesson 6: As a leader you must be able to deal with the 'tough' questions

Why Trumps' strategy of never answering a single question actually works

'The cornerstone of Trump's success in this campaign is his trademark attacks on anyone who crosses him. The brilliance of these attacks, regardless of how unpleasant or unpalatable any of us might find them, lies in the immediate validation they provide to so many people who are frustrated to the point of contempt for the dysfunctionality of Washington. And there is a very tangible benefit that Trump derives from them.

That benefit is the remarkably high level of deception that these attacks enable Trump to accomplish. He is consistently able to diminish others, while at the same time enjoying a means to escape from answering the important policy questions that would allow voters to evaluate his potential effectiveness.' (HOUSTON. 2016)

◆◆◆◆◆◆◆

[i]Trump ignored and obfuscated recount questions...
[ii]He claimed he won the popular vote but couldn't give any facts or evidence...

Trump bluff about the Comey tapes could be a crime, experts say

'Harvard Law professor Laurence Tribe says 'it could readily be viewed , as Trump himself conceded, as an effort to influence the 'due administration of justice' (SEAGER. 2017)

─────────────────────

It's a leaders JOB to be able to answer the tough questions - even if all he/she can say is 'wow that's great question - I'm going to have to think about that and get back to you - but I WILL get back to you.'

What is a real and arrogant abuse of power is to refuse to answer questions as in the simple question 'does the president believe in climate change?' Questions, that really do just require a yes or no response.

Not answering and keeping people hanging on is such a huge waste of everyone's time and energy.

No-one ever said that being a leader was easy. It will be impossible to please everyone; there will always be people who dislike you; disagree with you; want to pull you down. It comes with the territory.

Learn to rise above the angst; answer questions; stick to your vision and your values and if there are questions you can't answer, then treat that as a gift. Go somewhere quiet and reflect on the questions – they may even give you insight.

'Have a lot of respect for the responsibility journalists have to ask tough questions, to hold the administration accountable and to be advocates for the citizens of the United States.'

Josh Earnest

i. Steve Peoples and Todd Richond. Global News. Donald Trump ignoring recount questions, focused on shaping administration. 26/11/2016. http://globalnews.ca/news/3090277/donald-trump-ignoring-recount-questions-focused-on-shaping-administration/
ii. Editorial, BBC News. Trump claims millions voted illegally in presidential poll. 28/11/2016. http://www.bbc.com/news/world-us-canada-38126438

Lesson 7: Don't make stuff up – ever, ever, ever

Donald Trump Explains Sweden Terror Comment That Baffled a Nation

'After bewildering residents and officials of Sweden by [iii]suggesting Saturday that a terror-related incident had occurred over the weekend in the small Nordic nation, President Donald Trump attributed his comment to a Fox News interview with a conservative filmmaker.

"We've got to keep our country safe. You look at what's happening in Germany, you look at what's happening last night in Sweden," Trump told the crowd at his campaign-like rally in Florida on Saturday, critiquing Europe's refugee policies and complaining that his travel ban had suffered setbacks in court. "Sweden, who would believe this?"' (MCCAUSLAND. 2017)

If you the leader think it's OK to lie, to fabricate, or make stuff up, then it won't be long before the people you appoint think it's OK too.

The problem with an organization built on lies, is that eventually people see through them, your dishonesty will be exposed and you lose their trust. Remember that at the end of the day your reputation is really all you have. Once your reputation starts to erode, clients will begin to look elsewhere. Good employees will leave and even suppliers will go elsewhere to protect their business. In Trump's case, his base will be eroded.

And, it's not a case of 'if' the lies get exposed... but when and then what? Your reputation becomes as worthless as your word and you and your business will be TOAST.

When a leader behaves this way, too many talented people get caught up in the games; the cover-ups; the distractions; the retractions; the never ending dramas and eventual self inflicted witch-hunts.

So much time wasted; so much talent being wasted, so little getting done.

'A typical vice of American Politics is the avoidance of saying anything real on real issues.'
Theodore Roosevelt

Lesson 8: If you said it, own it

I was joking when I said the Chinese 'created' the concept of climate change

'I think that climate change is just a very, very expensive form of tax. A lot of people are making a lot of money. I know much about climate change," Trump said. "I've received many environmental awards. And I often joke that this is done for the benefit of China — obviously I joke — but this done for the benefit of China. Because China does not do anything to help climate change. They burn everything you can burn. They couldn't care less. Their standards are nothing. But in the meantime, they can undercut us on price. So it's very hard on our business.' (CAMPBELL. 2016)

♦♦♦♦♦♦♦

It wasn't MY idea!

'Mr. Trump has told four people close to him that he regrets going along with Speaker Paul D. Ryan's plan to push a health care overhaul before unveiling a tax cut proposal more politically palatable to Republicans. He said ruefully this week that he should have done tax reform first when it became clear that the quick-hit health care victory he had hoped for was not going to materialize on Thursday, the seventh anniversary of the act's passage, when the legislation was scheduled for a vote.' (LINKINS. 2017)

So it was all Paul Ryan's fault then? Another blame game in progress.

As TV host Lawrence O'Donnell quickly assessed, "Today was a big win for the president. The 44th president, Barack Obama, and it was, to put it in Trump-speak, a complete disaster for the current president. But Washington politics are different. Add in the Russia affair – the resignation of the president's national security adviser, groundless claims of wiretapping against Obama and an ongoing FBI investigation into his associates – and the first two months of the Trump presidency reek of chaos, crisis and confusion."

♦♦♦♦♦♦♦

Trump: I could 'shoot somebody and I wouldn't lose voters'

'Donald Trump boasted Saturday that support for his presidential campaign would not decline even if he shot someone in the middle of a crowded street. "I could stand in the middle of 5th Avenue and shoot somebody and I wouldn't lose voters.' (DIAMOND. 2016)

◆◆◆◆◆◆◆

Trump doesn't want a poor person running the US economy

'He said he loves all people but that rich people are better at handling money and would do better to steer the US economy.

Trump's Cabinet is filled with a number of billionaires, making it one of the wealthiest in US history.' (SETHI. 2017)

Throw away remarks are incredibly dangerous and can be the downfall of anyone in a leadership role. What is humorous to one person can be distinctly hurtful to another. What is said to impress one group of people, (in this case Trump's followers) can be the very thing that turns another group away from you.

And the most dangerous comment of all is a throw away remark that is made under pressure, such remarks can be a sign of what the speaker really thinks or feels on a given issue versus the sanitized version proposed by a speech writer or even legal advisor.

'There are plenty of recommendations on how to get out of trouble cheaply and fast. Most of them come down to this; deny your responsibility.'

L.B. Johnson -

Lesson 9: Saying something over and over and over again doesn't make it true

I Won the Popular Vote' if Illegal Voters Discounted

'In addition to winning the Electoral College in a landslide, I won the popular vote if you deduct the millions of people who voted illegally," Trump tweeted as reporters waited for him to leave his Mar-a-Lago golf resort in Florida to fly back to his residence in New York City.' (BREITBART NEWS. 2016)

The tragedy of comments like this are that their veracity can easily be verified:

- [i]Hillary won the popular vote by around 2.9 million.
- [ii]There is no evidence to suggest that there were 2.5 million Illegal voters

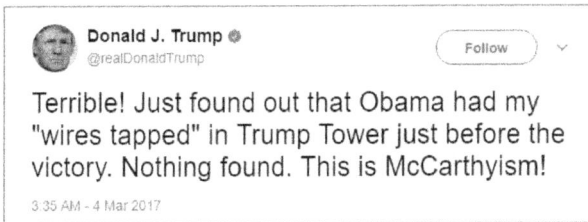

Donald J. Trump @
@realDonaldTrump

Follow

Terrible! Just found out that Obama had my "wires tapped" in Trump Tower just before the victory. Nothing found. This is McCarthyism!

3:35 AM - 4 Mar 2017

Back to fact checking. Even if we don't like what we find, as leaders we need to accept reality. The one thing Trump said over and over that was impressive – 'Make America Great Again', and this is what got him the job.

Well done Donald – you captured hearts and minds.

The problem is that his plan for doing this is destined to do the exact opposite, because it is just that, a catchy slogan. It doesn't appear to have any substance or strategy to make it come to fruition. You need more than a red hat and a slogan to run a country.

> 'A delusion is something that people believe in despite a total lack of evidence.'
>
> Richard Dawkins

---

i. Alana Abramson, ABC News 22/12/2016. Hillary Clinton officially wins popular vote by 2.9 million. http://abcnews.go.com/Politics/hillary-clinton-officially-wins-popular-vote-29-million/story?id=44354341
ii. Maggie Haberman et al, The New York Times 24/1/2017. Press Secretary Affirms that Trump Believes Lie of Millions of Illegal Voters. http://abcnews.go.com/Politics/hillary-clinton-officially-wins-popular-vote-29-million/story?id=44354341

Lesson 10: Some things are beyond 'spin'

The failure of the healthcare reform was a success

'So, if the bill goes down in defeat, it's a "100%" win. And if it passes, well, Trump will obviously take credit. Apparently the real "art of the deal" is finding a way to have it both ways.' (LINKINS. 2017)

———————————————

As leaders it is so vital that we think through to the end result of any initiative we put our names beside. To be very clear why we are changing something, and to have thought through all the possible outcomes, win or lose. To really ask the 'what if' questions before we implement anything.

In the case of the healthcare bill:

- What if, instead of dismantling, "we tweak and improve?"

- What if we look at the parts that are working and those that are not and discard or improve?

- What if what we are creating ends up being worse than the original?

- What if this idea falls flat on its face?

- Do we have a plan B?

As leaders embarking on any change process you need to be very clear as to why you are making the changes in the first place. And, you need to be brutally aware of the possible reactions and responses to possible failure.

The ability to admit you are wrong is probably the most courageous leadership skill of all.

"The reason I talk to myself is because I'm the only one whose answers I accept."
George Carlin

Lesson 11: If there is bad news to deliver YOU must be the person who delivers it.

Trump didn't mean wiretapping when he tweeted about wiretapping

'Spicer also said that Trump was referring to the Obama administration broadly -- and not accusing Obama of personal involvement -- when he tweeted that "Obama had my 'wires tapped' in Trump Tower" and accused Obama of being a "bad" or "sick guy."' (DIAMOND. 2017)

This is one of the absolute basics of leadership. If we learn nothing else it is that WE must own our own bad news. Asking someone else to do that for us borders on sad; tragic and gutless. Never embarrass yourself and humiliate your staff by expecting them to clean up after you.

Say what you mean and own it, (*see lesson 7*) because the day you start sending in minions to do your dirty work is the day respect for you will start to diminish on all fronts. It is also the day you should hand in your badge!

'Mistakes are always forgivable,
if you have the courage to admit them.'
Bruce Lee

Chapter 3

Set yourself up for small successes in the early days

"Why aren't crazy people content to take over, like, one town? It always has to be the whole world. They can't just control maybe twenty people. They have to control everyone. They can't just be stinking rich. They can't just do genetic experiments on a couple unlucky few. They have to put something in the water. In the air. To get everyone. I was tired of all of it."

James Patterson, Angel

Lesson 12: Have your finger on the pulse from day one

Trump Earns Majority Of Americans' Disapproval In Record Time

'Trump, barely two months into his presidency, is well within the "honeymoon period" that other presidents have enjoyed. Despite a wave of high-profile controversies and setbacks, including the failure of the Obamacare repeal bill, his White House has yet to face a recession, a major international incident or any sort of crisis beyond the self-inflicted.' (SPARKS. 2017)

You are the alpha and omega. Everything rests with you, so If you are suffering crises in the early days, learn to identify the causes and be prepared to change tack quickly. It doesn't mean you lose sight of your ultimate goal, it simply means you need to get some early runs on the board. Doing this sends some strong messages; it says you are 'listening,' and in touch with your people.

It's ok to take time, to settle in.

WARNING: If the crises that surround you are caused by you then STOP whatever it is you are doing to create the chaos. Seek advice from people who have gone before you.

Sadly, some people literally thrive on drama. If they experience a day without some form of melt-down they worry.... they don't feel alive. Don't be one of these leaders. It will shorten your life and stress out your followers.

"If you ask the CEO of some major corporation what he does he will say, in all honesty, that he is slaving 20 hours a day to provide his customers with the best goods or services he can and creating the best possible working conditions for his employees. But then you take a look at what the corporation does, the effect of its legal structure, the vast inequalities in pay and conditions, and you see the reality is something far different."

Noam Chomsky

Lesson 13: Pick your first few fights very carefully

Trump's first major test as travel ban uproar spreads

'The measures, introduced just a week after he took office, have been criticized by allies, caused confusion among border guards and galvanized Democrats looking for a way to bash Trump. There was also growing unease among Republican lawmakers to the move. Four federal judges moved to halt deportations, around 300 people were stopped or detained worldwide and US civil rights lawyers warned the battle could head to the Supreme Court.' (MATTHEWS. 2017)

So just one week into the job, Trump not only had America in an uproar, he had

the whole world in an uproar.

♦♦♦♦♦♦♦

Trump's Second Travel Ban is Blocked by Two US Judges

"Once again, a judge cited Trump's remarks on the campaign trail as an indication of his intent to keep Muslims out of the country. Watson, in Honolulu, pointed to the president's plainly worded statements before the election, saying they "betray the executive order's stated secular purpose," while the real motive was "temporarily suspending the entry of Muslims."' (MEHROTRA. 2017)

Yes, it's great to want to achieve results in a new role; it's great to have a vision and a plan, but causing an uproar in the first few weeks of a new position does not bode well for going forward if you want to take people with you.

Learn the ropes; get to know people; test the water. Run things past people who have more experience than you. Get some of the easier and smaller issues out of the way first before you deal with the bigger issues.

Your followers want and need some successes in the early days too – they want to know they have aligned themselves with the right leader!

Before you assume, learn
Before you judge, understand
Before you hurt, feel
Before you say, think.

Not known

Lesson 14: Don't delude yourself

Out of his depth, Donald Trump clings to deception

'When confronted with his claim that global warming was a hoax perpetrated by the Chinese, Trump replied, "I did not [say it]." He did. When Trump's claim that he could not release his tax returns because of an IRS audit was exposed as false, he still insisted on it. When charged with saying that he could personally negotiate down the national debt, he said this was "wrong." The charge was right. When Trump's transparently deceptive claim to be an early opponent of the Iraq War was debunked, he doubled down in a babbling defense citing Sean Hannity as the ultimate arbiter. It is not surprising that Trump inhabits his own factual universe, in which truth is determined by usefulness and lies become credible through repetition. What made the first presidential debate extraordinary — really, unprecedented — was not the charges that Trump denied, but the ones he confirmed.' (GERSON. 2016)

◆◆◆◆◆◆◆

Here Is Trump's Absurd Defence For His Wiretap Claim

'I have my own form of media," the president replied. "So if I tweet two or three or four or five times a day, and if most of them are good, and I really want them all to be good, but if I make one mistake in a month — this one I don't think is going to prove to be a mistake at all.' (FANG. 2017)

◆◆◆◆◆◆◆

President Trump's thoroughly confusing Fox Business interview annotated

'TRUMP: Well, look, you know because you cover it. We've done an amazing job on regulations. We've freed it up. We freed up this country so much, the miners and energy and the banking system is now coming, too, with Dodd-Frank, which is a disaster. We freed up so much and we're getting great, great credit for it. We have done so much for so many people. I don't think that there is a presidential period of time in the first 100 days where anyone has done nearly what we've been able to do.' (BLAKE. 2017)

◆◆◆◆◆◆◆

Trump: 'I can't be doing so badly, because I'm president and you're not'

'In a wide-ranging interview with Time magazine, President Donald Trump defended his controversial statements on wiretapping, voter fraud and an array of other issues, claiming he has ultimately been proven right time and time again. "I'm a very instinctual person, but my instinct turns out to be right," Trump told Time's Washington bureau chief Michael Scherer in an interview conducted Wednesday and published Thursday morning. "I tend to be right. I'm an instinctual person, I happen to be a person that knows how life works."

To support his claim, Trump pointed to his prediction that Britain would vote to leave the European Union, his insistence that NATO member states meet their defense spending obligations when "nobody knew that they weren't paying" and his shocking victory in the presidential election itself as proof that he is often proven right. But Trump also pointed to more dubious examples, including his mysterious reference during a February rally to some unspecified event that happened "last night in Sweden" when nothing had happened in the Scandinavian country the night before. The White House later sought to clarify that Trump had been speaking generally about rising crime in Sweden, not a specific event, but in his Time interview, Trump said he had been vindicated by riots that broke out in Stockholm two days after his "last night" remark.' (NELSON. 2017)

We've already said it's NOT OK to make 'stuff' up but delusions take a leader into a whole new realm of NOT OK.

If a leader seriously thinks they are doing a great job when all the people around them and the various success indicators suggest they are NOT, then putting a 'spin' on things ultimately serves no purpose.

In Trump's case, unbelievably, he seems to get away with it. I would imagine that if such thinking and beliefs and comments came from the CEO of a publicly listed company, that CEO would have about 5 minutes to clear their desk and hop into the taxi waiting at the door to take them off to create havoc and despair somewhere else.

... Surely?

As a leader, you must be able to be honest with yourself.

Surround yourself with people who will challenge you and hold you accountable; people who won't let you off the hook if they think you are going off track.

No-one is asking a leader to bend with the wind or to try and please everyone, but don't delude yourself that you walk on water; or that you are God's gift to business or the world.

You are not.

> "How Come Every Time I Get Stabbed in the Back,
> My Fingerprints Are on the Knife?"
> Jerry B. Harvey (Author)

Chapter 4

Build on the work of your predecessor

"Don't ever take a fence down until you know why it was put up."

Robert Frost

Lesson 15: It makes no sense to simply keep undoing everything your predecessor put in place

Poll: Most Americans Say Don't Repeal Obamacare Without A Replacement.

'An overwhelming majority of people disapprove of Republican lawmakers' plan to repeal the Affordable Care Act without having a ready replacement for the health care law, according to a poll released Friday.

A poll released Friday by the Kaiser Family Foundation finds that 75 percent of Americans say they either want lawmakers to leave Obamacare alone, or repeal it only when they can replace it with a new health care law. Twenty percent of those polled say they want to see the law killed immediately.' (KODJAK. 2017)

And judging by the letter-writing and lobbying in the first week of the new congressional session, many health care and business groups agree.

◆◆◆◆◆◆◆

Coal country Republicans cut state mine inspections

'A bill approved by Kentucky lawmakers Tuesday would cut back the number of state inspections of coal mines per year. It would allow the state's Department of Natural Resources to substitute some of those safety inspections with what's known as safety analyses. Conveniently for coal operators, the analyses do not pose the threat of citations and fines.' (JAMIESON. 2017)

◆◆◆◆◆◆◆

Trump signs bill making it easier for employers to hide worker injuries

'Republicans just repealed a major safety regulation issued by former President Barack Obama. By scuttling a rule issued by former President Barack Obama, Trump and Republicans in Congress have effectively shortened the amount of time that employers in dangerous industries can be required to keep accurate records of worker injuries — from five years to just six months.' (JAMIESON. 2017)

◆◆◆◆◆◆◆

Republicans may be making a mistake by swinging only for the fences

'Legislative successes have come on small bills that wiped out regulations from the last weeks President Obama was in office. Lawmakers are using the obscure Congressional Review Act to do so on party-line votes. Those dozens of nixed regulations do represent a win for Trump, and Republican leaders are aware of the need to demonstrate some wins. In an interview before Congress left for its two-week spring break, Senate Majority Leader Mitch McConnell (R-Ky.) noted that undoing regulations "unfortunately doesn't make a lot of news" and said his office was going to compile a report on the sweep and impact of those moves.' (KANE. 15/4/2017)

◆◆◆◆◆◆◆

Trump praises Australia's universal health care after Obamacare repeal

'US Senator Bernie Sanders quickly picked up on the remark which came after Trump's new bill passed by a handful of votes. The new law still has to pass the US Senate. "Well Mr President, you're right, in Australia and every other major country on Earth they guarantee health care to all people. They don't throw 24 million people off health insurance. So maybe when we get to the Senate we should start off with looking at the Australian health care system.' (WESTCOTT. 2017)

NB: Australia has a universal health care system, known as Medicare, which gives citizens free access to doctors and public hospitals paid for by the government.

――――――――――――――――――――――――

Don't undo people's lives to make yourself look good and feel good. Don't undo everything that's good about what is already in place and even if, as a leader, you think something set up by a predecessor IS broken, take some time to find out where, why and how to make changes. Trashing and crashing everything your predecessor did may give you glow but may do nothing to improve the final outcome - you will have trashed something that sort of worked for something that absolutely doesn't.

Think about how that will reflect on you. Take time to change things; in fact, the more important an issue is (and I don't think there could be anything more important to the ordinary American than their health care) then the longer you should take.

Until a leader has been in a role for a while and acquired a 'feel' for the organization, a whole lot of 'listening' needs to take place before decisions are made. Sometimes doing the opposite of what everyone else is doing is a good idea; sometimes it is NOT; sometimes things are done a certain way because they actually work.

Check also your rationale for wanting to change something. Is it just to make your mark? Is it to prove your predecessor wrong or is it because you genuinely believe the existing system needs replacing?

Which then begs the question – does it need to be replaced in its entirety or are there tweaks that could be made to make the system more effective and efficient.

What is amazing is that every country is faced with the same health-care challenges; an aging population; people living longer; technology that can cure people but a lack funds to do so. How come it seems that only America has such a massive challenge looking after the health of their people?

Never be afraid to use other people's ideas. Investigate other country's healthcare programs. Why re-invent the wheel? And in America's case; don't make health care a political football – surely this should be a bi-partisan issue?

Are Trump and the Republican Party doing it because:

- They genuinely believe that Obama did a bad job?

- It wasn't their idea?

- It uses the word 'Obama' - though of course it is actually called 'Affordable Health Care'?

- It gives too much help to people on low income and how dare they expect any sort of help?

- It's pure politics?

- It's pure spite?

- It's racial?

Change for change sake can be another of those dumb mistakes.

Whatever their rationale is it makes the Republican party and Trump look mean spirited and out of touch with reality. And the $64,000 question - what it is going to do to those 20 - 24 million people who will no longer have any kind of health insurance?

That doesn't actually bear thinking about.

Shame on them.

"If it ain't broke, don't fix it."
T.Bert

NB: T. Bert (Thomas Bertram) Lance, the Director of the Office of Management and Budget in Jimmy Carter's 1977 administration. He was quoted in the newsletter of the US Chamber of Commerce, Nation's Business, May 1977.

Lesson 16: Give credit where credit is due to your predecessor

GOP Senator Concedes Democrats Had A Better Process When Passing Health Care Law

'In their seven-year effort to repeal the ACA, the GOP frequently claimed former President Barack Obama and Democrats rushed through their bill. In reality, Obama and his aides spent more than a year working on specific proposals, meeting with various experts and stakeholders and convening a bipartisan group of lawmakers to gather ideas and feedback.

By contrast, Trump spent only a few weeks on the GOP bill, even though Republicans have promised for seven years to repeal Obamacare.' (FANG. 2017)

◆◆◆◆◆◆◆

A bit of 'fact checking' by the incoming administration (though I'm pretty sure they would have known this) would have revealed the following:

"When the Democrats came to power in 2009, for 60 years at least, they had been pursuing a national healthcare system, yet they didn't introduce legislation for eight months, and they didn't pass it for over a year of Barack Obama's first term. Obama and his aides spent more than a year working on specific proposals, meeting with various experts and stakeholders and convening a bipartisan group of lawmakers to gather ideas and feedback." Sen. Tom Cotton (R-Ark.)

He went on to say: "it went through very public hearings and took testimony, developed fact based foundation of knowledge, President Obama travelled around the country, held town halls and spoke to a joint session of Congress," the senator added. "I am not saying we needed 14 months to do this, but I think a more careful and deliberate approach, which we now have time to do because we are going to have to revisit healthcare anyway, would have gotten us further down the path to a solution. I think you can't expect to try to solve a problem that addresses one-sixth of the country's economy and touches every American in a very personal and intimate way."

Acknowledge your predecessor; thank them for a job well done – even if you think they haven't done the job well. Bad mouthing the person or people that have gone before you just makes you look sad, nasty and vindictive.

I know in Trump's case we are talking 'politics' and I know that in politics it isn't done to credit the other party, which is a shame. Imagine how refreshing it would be if the next generation of voters heard politicians actually giving credit to great ideas no matter which party they came from. It may even give politicians a better image with the public and wouldn't that be a giant leap for mankind?

But if nothing else, in a leadership role, whether political or not, don't trash the person who has gone before you - it says nothing about them and everything about you!

'Praise the bridge that carried you over.'
George Colman

Lesson 17: Don't take credit for the hard work your predecessor did

Republicans Are Suddenly Thrilled About The Jobs Report

'President Donald Trump and other Republicans were quick to tout Friday's job report showing the U.S. economy added 235,000 jobs in February, but it's worth looking at how they responded to similar good economic news under President Barack Obama.

Friday's jobs report, which showed unemployment at 4.7 percent, signals that the U.S. economy is moving in the right direction. But there have now been 77 consecutive months of job growth. When good job numbers came out under the Obama administration, Trump and other Republicans would undermine them by highlighting certain slow areas or suggesting that the numbers did not reflect an accurate picture of the American economy.

Trump has long claimed that the unemployment rate released in the monthly jobs report is artificially low, saying, inaccurately, in 2015 that it could be as high as 42 percent. Trump has argued that the unemployment number is misleading because it doesn't consider the number of people who have stopped looking for work, but even if you do include that figure, the numbers are nowhere close to what Trump claims.

Despite Trump's uncertainty about the unemployment rate, White House advisers and Republicans were quick to tout it Friday.' (LEVINE. 2017)

This is another of those scenarios where in politics you would never praise your predecessor even if results were built on their hard work. What a different language politicians could use; what a different perception that would give to people about politics and their representatives.

Surely leadership is about building on what has gone before not trashing it? Even if the best you can do is say 'nothing', then that is still better than taking praise that you have not earned.

> "Be modest in your behaviour if you really want to overcome arrogance.
> If you boast about your achievements and praise yourself
> you will look dumb. If you have done something that is praise worthy,
> then let others decide."
> Dr Anil Kumar Sinha

Chapter 5

Watch for early warning signs that things are going off track

'You can avoid reality, but you cannot avoid the consequences of avoiding reality.'

Ayn Rand

Lesson 18: There WILL be obvious signs that your leadership is in crisis

Donald Trump's First Presidential Approval Ratings Are a Record Low

'Trump is the first elected U.S. president to start out with a job approval rating below 50% in the history of Gallup surveys, which date back to Dwight D. Eisenhower in 1953. Just 45% of respondents said they approve of the job Trump is doing, while 45% disapprove, according to a Gallup poll.' (REILLY. 2017)

♦♦♦♦♦♦♦

Until Trump Decides Otherwise, A Bloc Of House Conservatives Now Controls Government

'This will hopefully be a learning moment for President Trump, especially when you look ahead at other big issues like tax reform, the debt ceiling and infrastructure," said Brian Walsh, a longtime Republican operative.' (GRIM. 2017)

At the time of writing this chapter, Trump hadn't even reached his first 100 days! To date, Trump has failed to:

- Implement the first travel ban.
- Implement the 2nd travel ban.
- Implement Healthcare Reform
- Put Hillary in jail.
- Find proof of wire-tapping.
- Build that wall.

The tragedy for a president is that the approval ratings for all previous presidents are on record, so even within days of Trump taking office his ratings were being unfavorably compared.

As a CEO or business leader, it takes longer for your approval ratings to settle, unless you've entered into a business already in crisis. That said, you are granted a degree of latitude to assess, plan and implement strategy. Even so, shareholders will have their finger on the pulse of the promises you've made, and they will be keeping score of the results you are achieving against those promises.

Take ratings seriously. Don't gloss over them because at some stage they will affect your ability to lead and they WILL speed up your demise.

As a leader reading this take the time to re-read Chapter 3. Set yourself up for small successes because if the cracks are showing and you still stubbornly persist in following the same track, then the end will be right around the corner.

We all need to be willing to take a deep breath and take some time out to have a rethink.

It's OK to do that, 'Rome really wasn't built in a day.'

"Now this is not the end. It is not even the beginning of the end.
But it is, perhaps, the end of the beginning.'
Winston Churchill

Lesson 19: Don't lavish money on yourself before you invest it in your followers: they will never forgive you; they will never forget and in the end there will be a day of reckoning

How many of us have worked for organizations where the leader has explained the necessity to tighten our belts; to pull back on pay rises and to halt all investment in social activities only to watch that self same leader drive into work one morning in a brand new, very expensive company car?

Imagine how that makes our followers feel. Imagine our reaction when that same leader then asks us to work overtime (whilst on salary) or to cut our hours for the good of the company.

Shame on these types of leaders.

◆◆◆◆◆◆◆

How Much Do Trump Mar-A-Lago Trips Cost? He's Burning A Hole In Taxpayers' Pockets

'It appears that Trumps' trips to Mar-A-Lago cost roughly $1 million per trip. A comparable outing to Florida by former President Barack Obama cost only $586,000. According to the conservative watchdog group Judicial Watch, taxpayers spent around $96 million on Obama's travel expenses over the course of eight years. If Trump continues at his current pace, then, he will rack up more travel costs in his first year than Obama did during his entire presidency.' (MILLSTEIN. 2017)

◆◆◆◆◆◆◆

The estimated $58 million annual cost to protect Trump Tower alone would pay for:

- 7.1 million home-delivered meals to senior citizens; OR

- More than 720 new teachers; OR

- Shelter for more than 15,500 families for one month; OR

- Resurfacing nearly 390 miles of road
  (MOSENDZ. 2017)

◆◆◆◆◆◆◆

Tracking the President's Visits to Trump Properties

'In his first 229 days in office he spent 75 of those days at Trump properties and 1 in every 5 days at his own golf resorts. This from a man who said he never took holidays and would keep his business separate from the presidency.' (YOURISH, GRIGGS. 5/9/2017)

Any new leader may be tempted to spend up large in their early days; to reward their promotion with some nice new furniture or a shiny new car. It probably seems especially OK to do this if they have inherited a healthy surplus.

Sooner or later though, the books have to be reconciled: sooner or later the people who are being short-changed so you can live the good life will turn on you.

Leaders must always keep their eye on where they are spending money; where they are cutting it and the impression that gives to their followers. It won't take the American people long to work out that Donald and his family are living very well off the public coffers. Watch that worm turn in the mid-terms.

Always put your followers first and yourself last. It will pay massive dividends in the long run.

'You can fool some of the people all of the time,
and all of the people some of the time,
but you cannot fool all of the people all of the time.'
Abraham Lincoln

Lesson 20: Be very clear what you are 'measuring' and why

We can't spend money on programs just because they sound good: Trump budget would slash funding from Meals on Wheels

'President Donald Trump's proposed budget, unveiled on Thursday, would cut federal funding for Meals on Wheels, a program that provides daily meals to millions of low-income seniors across the country. White House Office of Management and Budget Director Mick Mulvaney told reporters at a press conference Thursday that Meals on Wheels "sounds great." But he said that along with other anti-poverty programs, it is "not showing any results.' (RELMAN. 2017)

◆◆◆◆◆◆◆

Trump Gives States The Okay To Defund Planned Parenthood

'Now, states can withhold federal family planning grants from providers because they offer abortion, even though the longstanding Hyde Amendment prevents any federal money from being used to pay for abortion. The Senate narrowly passed the resolution at the end of March after Vice President Mike Pence was summoned to break a tie vote. Two Republicans, Sens. Susan Collins (Maine) and Lisa Murkowski (Alaska), broke with their party and opposed the measure.

"If you're serious about trying to reduce the number of abortions," Collins said after the vote, "the best way to do that is to make family planning more widely available."

The Title X federal family planning program, established by President Richard Nixon in 1970, subsidizes contraception, Pap smears and other preventative health care services for 4 million low-income Americans, roughly half of whom are uninsured. Planned Parenthood uses the $70 million it receives in Title X grants a year to serve 1.5 million patients — about one-third of the patients in the program.' (BASSETT. 2017)

Consider cause and effect. All businesses measure their bottom line; that's a given. But sometimes bottom line results are misleading. Leaders can measure the wrong things. Sometimes leaders put their energy into measuring one aspect of their business (like sales) and forget that increasing sales may actually cause a 'cost' somewhere else, i.e. we sell more 'stuff' but end up with customer complaints because we are either unable to 'deliver' the goods on time or we allow quality to suffer in order to maintain delivery schedules.

The Trump budget is going to take resources away from many of America's elderly; the very hard working people who voted for him and working families just trying to get by and most devastating of all is that it will massively hit the very poor.

In the case of meals-on-wheels and the comment that they are not showing any 'results,' my question would have to be 'what results were you expecting from delivering meals-on-wheels to the elderly?' Is it that they are not dying quickly enough and so if we stop feeding them they will pass off the mortal coil a bit faster as a result of starvation and we could then what: put the people who were delivering the food to better use?

Similarly, the Trump budget is going to:

- Make it impossible for around [i]24 million people in America to get health insurance.

- Get rid of after school care for [ii]1.6 million kids whose parents need that care so they can work.

- Cut programs for [iii]disabled kids.

- Cut food aid to [iv]40 million children around the world in the poorest countries.

Didn't he say he would make America Great Again? Aren't these the very people who heard that? Aren't these the very people who voted for him? Aren't these the very people he will hurt the most? Won't these be the very people who will turn against Trump and the Republican Party?

"Compassion is the basis of morality."
Arthur Schopenhauer -

i. Dan Mangan, CNBC 14/3/2017. 24 million would lose health insurance coverage under GOP's Obamacare replacement by 2026. https://finance.yahoo.com/news/24-million-lose-health-insurance-203447129.html
ii. Emma Brown, The Washington Post 16/3/2017. Trump budget casualty: After-school programs for 1.6 million kids. Most are poor. https://www.washingtonpost.com/local/education/trump-budget-casualty-afterschool-programs-for-16-million-kids-most-are-poor/2017/03/16/78802430-0a6f-11e7-b77c-0047d15a24e0_story.html?utm_term=.1646a706b655
iii. Miles Archer, Democratic Underground 12/3/2017. Trump Budget: aid for disabled children, hot meals for elderly cut to pay for a military buildup. https://upload.democraticunderground.com/10028783913
iv. News, Oregonlive 20/3/2017. Trump budget cuts off food aid for millions of kids in the world's poorest places. http://www.oregonlive.com/today/index.ssf/2017/03/trump_budget_cuts_off_food_hel.html

Lesson 21: Spending money and cutting money

Trump on pace to surpass 8 years of Obama's travel spending in
1 year

'Donald Trump's travel to his private club in Florida has cost over an estimated $20 million in his first 80 days as president, putting the president on pace in his first year of office to surpass former President Barack Obama's spending on travel for his entire eight years.

The outsized spending on travel stands in stark relief to Trump's calls for belt tightening across the federal government and the fact that he regularly criticized Obama for costing the American taxpayer money every time he took a trip.' (MERICA. 2017)

◆◆◆◆◆◆◆

Cost of Trump family security vexes New York and Florida officials

'Senator Chuck Schumer of New York has ramped up pressure on Donald Trumpand the federal government to accept the mounting costs of protecting the president, the first family and their extended entourage. Schumer, the Senate Democratic leader, inserted himself into the debate on Sunday, saying it costs $500,000 per day for nearly 200 police officers to protect Trump Tower on Fifth Avenue in Manhattan, which houses the Trump family business headquarters and serves as the home of the first lady, Melania Trump, and the couple's son, Barron. The senator estimated the cost could rise to as much as $183m annually.

At current estimates, even a four-year Trump administration could be heading for a billion dollars in taxpayer-borne costs – an eight-fold increase of the $97m Judicial Watch, a conservative watchdog group, estimates it cost to protect Barack Obama over the two terms of his administration.' (HELMORE. 2017)

◆◆◆◆◆◆◆

Ivanka Trump's family skiing 'funded by the taxpayer'

'Taxpayers can't afford Meals on Wheels anymore, but they can afford to pay for Trump's kids to vacation,' says critic. Another anonymous law enforcement source said roughly 100 Secret Service agents were expected to accompany the family.' (OPPENHEIM. 2017)

◆◆◆◆◆◆◆

Trump's Education Budget Revealed

'Trump's budget plan would remove $2.4 billion in grants for teacher training and $1.2 billion in funding for summer- and after-school programs. It also curtails or eliminates funding for around 20 departmental programs "that are not effective, that duplicate other efforts, or that do not serve national needs."' (BENDIX. 2017)

◆◆◆◆◆◆◆

The cost of Betsy DeVos's security detail — nearly $8 million over nearly 8 months

'Federal marshals are protecting Education Secretary Betsy DeVos at a cost to her agency of nearly $8 million over nearly eight months, according to the U.S. Marshals Service.' (BROWN, BARRETT. 2017)

◆◆◆◆◆◆◆

Trump has visited a Trump branded property every 2.8 days of his presidency

'For the 10th weekend in a row, President Trump is visiting a Trump-branded property — every weekend except the first two after his inauguration. For the sixth weekend in a row, he's golfing at one of those properties; he's golfed on nine of those 10 weekends. In total, Trump has spent time at one or more Trump-branded properties on 28 of the days he's been president — meaning that he visits a property that's part of his private business empire more than one-third of the days he's been in office, or once every 2.8 days. The frequency at which he golfs is lower: He's golfed on 17.9 percent of the days he's been president, or about once every 5.6 days.' (BUMP. 2017)

◆◆◆◆◆◆◆

As The Trumps Travel, The Secret Service Can't Even Afford To Pay Some Agents

'It's no secret that President Donald Trump's penchant for weekend getaways has created added costs for the Secret Service. But the agency is in such dire straits that more than 1,000 agents have hit the caps for annual salary and over-time allowances, director Randolph "Tex" Alles told USA Today in an exclusive interview.' (FREJ. 2017)

◆◆◆◆◆◆◆

- Image is everything...

- Perception is reality...

- Keep your hands out of the till...

- Stop spending money that isn't yours...

- Stop spending money on yourself that you have taken from the poorer members of your business/electorate...

- Don't make your company or country bankrupt...

The tragedy here is that Jared Kushner, Ivanka Trump, Donald Trump (allegedly, because we don't really know his worth due to his refusal to release his tax returns) and DeVos are all billionaires. They don't need to gorge on the public trough.

"Earth provides enough to satisfy every man's needs,
but not every man's greed."
Mahatma Gandhi

Lesson 22: Chart a clear and concise path. If you are confused everyone around you will be confused

We don't know where Trump stands. Neither does he.

'So much for Donald Trump, the "America First" populist champion of the forgotten working class. The president now sounds pretty much like a garden-variety globalist, defending the "rigged" system he denounced during the campaign. Then again, who knows how he'll sound next week? He hasn't even been in office for three full months, and Trump may already be the most erratic president we've ever seen. We have no idea where he really stands because, well, neither does he.' (ROBINSON. 2017)

◆◆◆◆◆◆◆

President Trump, King of flip-flops

'Sometimes, it was difficult to determine his actual positions amid the flipping and flopping. On the minimum wage, in particular, he was on so many sides that no matter what he position he took as president, he could claim he was consistent with a previously held stance.

When you're running for president, or when you're watching politics on the sidelines as a reality TV star or businessman, it's easy to lob baseless rhetoric. Many of Trump's recent flip-flops appeared to result from being confronted with facts he needs to accept to conduct diplomacy, or make decisions as commander in chief. As in the words of "Hamilton" the musical: "Winning was easy ... governing is harder."

'On NATO being "obsolete". Throughout the campaign, and as recently as March 22, Trump declared the trans-Atlantic alliance "obsolete, because it doesn't cover terrorism." Of course, this was factually incorrect: NATO has been involved in counterterrorism since 1980, and especially since 9/11. I complained about that a long time ago and they made a change, and now they do fight terrorism. I said it was obsolete. It's no longer obsolete."

On the USA paying the 'lion's share' of contributions to Nato. "we are getting ripped off by every country in NATO, where they pay virtually nothing." As we previously explained, under guidelines established in 2006, defense expenditures of NATO alliance countries should amount to 2 percent of each country's gross domestic product by 2024. Trump stood by his inaccurate point about cost-sharing at the news conference: "I did ask about all the money that hasn't been paid over the years — will that money be coming back? We'll be talking about that."

On labeling China a currency manipulator. On April 12, Trump announced he would not label China a currency manipulator, breaking a key economic campaign promise. Throughout the campaign, and as recently as 10 days before this announcement, Trump falsely blamed China for being a "world champion" of devaluing the yuan. We rated that outdated claim Four Pinocchios: Not only is the United States not being hurt by China's current currency manipulation, China also is not devaluing its currency anymore. In fact, China is selling foreign currency to prop up its own, in an effort to prevent the yuan from depreciating further and destabilizing the Chinese and global economy. Yet on April 2, Trump insisted to the Financial Times that "our country hasn't had a clue, they haven't had a clue" about China's alleged currency manipulations.

On whether he knows Putin. On April 12, Trump claimed: "I don't know Putin." But as recently as November 2015, Trump repeatedly claimed he not only knew Vladimir Putin, but knew him "very well," and that he had a relationship with the Russian president. Trump changed his stance in July 2016, while facing criticism about his relationship with Kremlin: He declared he didn't know Putin, after all. Our colleague Philip Bump compiled a chronology of Trump's claims about Putin.

On intervening in Syria. Lastly, here's a bonus flip-flop that we previously covered in our running list of Trump's false or misleading claims in his first 100 days. On April 6, Trump authorized the launch of 59 cruise missiles at a Syrian military airfield in response to a chemical attack that killed dozens of civilians. It marked the first direct American military action against Syrian President Bashar al-Assad's regime since the country's civil war began. But in more than a dozen tweets in 2013 and 2014, Trump consistently opposed U.S. military action and urged then-President Barack Obama against launching air attacks on Syria for allegedly deploying chemical weapons. Trump said the United States should focus on domestic issues instead. Later, this view would evolve into the noninterventionist "America-first" platform of Trump's 2016 presidential campaign. Trump also mocked Obama for declaring a "red line," or Obama's threat to take U.S. military action if Syria used chemical weapons.' (LEE. 2017)

◆◆◆◆◆◆◆

The U.S. Military Thinks Missiles And Bombs Work Better With A Strategy, Too. They would like to know Trump's intent in North Korea, Syria and elsewhere.

'After 15 years of bloody, inconclusive war in Iraq and Afghanistan, experienced military officers are looking to President Donald Trump not just to pull the trigger on military action when needed. They're looking for a coherent statement of American goals and a coordinated strategy that combines military force with economic, political, diplomatic, cyber and media power — and doesn't leave the war to the military alone. "There is a limit, I think, to what we can do," Defense Secretary Jim Mattis said this week at a Pentagon news conference, when asked about next steps the military might take in Syria following the April 7 missile attack.' (WOOD. 2017)

♦♦♦♦♦♦♦

Want to change Trump's mind on policy? Be the last one who talks to him

'You can say this for President Trump: Unlike most other politicians, he's totally at peace with changing his mind at any given moment, with very little explanation. But where are these sudden changes coming from? Is it for a desire to moderate his populist policies? Is he suddenly reading briefing books? Or could it be that the president simply amenable to the last person he talked to? On that last point, we've noticed that some of his biggest flip-flops on a key issue of his issue happen immediately after he's talked to a person directly involved on the other side.' (PHILLIPS. 2017)

These situations keep on taking us back to Lesson 3: Know when you have reached the top of your game – or more succinctly – know when you are out of your depth.

The tragedy here is that America has this man for 4 years or worse if he is re-elected (surely not) for 8 years. Imagine the devastation his lack of direction; lack of protocol; lack of diplomacy; lack of any kind of understanding or even the desire for understanding the enormous challenges he needs to face and make, at the very least, some meaningful decisions that show some resemblance of direction.

Sadly the cracks are already showing, and as a result America is not one single step closer to 'being great again' - far from it.

Perhaps the real lesson here is that America's selection process for choosing their top person is flawed.

The 'people' got it right - they went for Hillary - and whether you like Hillary or not, she would not have created the havoc that Trump is causing within America or the embarrassment he is causing with leaders around the world.

So could this be a turning point for America; could/should the Electoral College be scrapped? They had a chance to say 'this man is not right for this role' but because of party politics and vested interests, they enabled this man to have the nuclear codes.

'If you do not know where you come from, then you don't know where you are, and if you don't know where you are, then you don't know where you're going. And if you don't know where you're going, you're probably going wrong."

Terry Pratchett, I Shall Wear Midnight

Lesson 23: Be aware your credibility is under constant scrutiny

Washington Post's David Fahrenthold wins Pulitzer Prize for dogged reporting of Trump's philanthropy

'Washington Post reporter David Fahrenthold remembers being struck by Donald Trump's pledge to donate $6 million, including $1 million of his personal funds, to veterans groups during a televised fundraiser before the Iowa caucuses early last year. Did Trump follow through? he wondered. So, weeks after the event, Fahrenthold started asking questions.

For several months, he found, the answer was no, despite assurances to the contrary from Trump's campaign. When Trump finally made the donation in late May, the reporter set off on a broader inquiry. In a detailed series of articles, he found that many of Trump's philanthropic claims over the years had been exaggerated and often were not truly charitable activities at all.' (FAHL. 2017)

◆◆◆◆◆◆◆

Trump's inauguration crowd: Sean Spicer's claims versus the evidence

'"We had 250,000 people literally around in the little ball we constructed." In other words, 250,000 people had been given tickets to the swearing-in ceremony, which is what the Joint Congressional Committee for Inaugural Ceremonies told CNN."

"The rest of the 20-block area, all the way back to the Washington monument was packed," Trump claimed.' (KLEIN. 2017)

This is an exaggeration. Photos taken at 12:09 pm, just after Trump was sworn in, show the crowd thinning closer to the Washington Monument:

◆◆◆◆◆◆◆

He promised to make US companies pay dearly for sending jobs overseas and/or for having goods made overseas – yet he continues to have products made overseas:

Report: Dozens of Trump products made overseas

'Donald Trump has been off-shoring the production of Trump brand products since 2006 despite his unrelenting criticism of companies that send jobs overseas.'

◆◆◆◆◆◆◆

Time Asks Donald Trump To Remove Fake Cover From Business Properties

'Time on Tuesday asked the Trump Organization to remove any fake covers of the magazine displayed at the presidential family's business properties.

The magazine's request to the group came after a Washington Post report revealed that several of President Donald Trump's golf courses had a framed copy of a doctored Time cover, which featured the commander in chief as the cover story.'

Sadly some leaders tend to think they live in a bubble; a bubble where no-one can see what they are doing or check what they are saying.

Big lesson – You are on the stage being watched every minute of every day.

Do what you say you will do. Check your facts, always, every time and forever.

'Never expect loyalty from a person who
can't give you honesty'
Surgeo Bell

Lesson 24: Does credibility even matter?

Top Election Officials Have No Idea What Trump Is Planning To Do In His Voter Fraud Investigation

'Despite insistence that widespread voter fraud exists and pledges to investigate the matter fully, it seems the Trump administration has not bothered to contact top state election officials across the country. The Huffington Post asked all 50 secretaries of state and election officials in the District of Columbia if they had been contacted by the White House or Department of Justice regarding the forthcoming investigation. Not a single secretary of state's office responded to say that it had.' (LEVINE. 2017)

◆◆◆◆◆◆◆

Trump's credibility is shot

'Monday was a turning point for Donald Trump's credibility. He had fibbed about crowd numbers, and pushed crazy conspiracy stories about illegal voters. But continuing to claim that former President Obama ordered the wiretapping of Trump Tower, even after the sitting FBI and NSA directors made clear it was false, was a new low.' (PSAKI. 2017)

◆◆◆◆◆◆◆

Trump Administration Won't Release Logs Of Visitors To The White House

'The decision is a departure from the Obama administration, which did release the logs. Michael Dubke, the White House communications director, told Time that the White House's decision was made out of concern for national security and privacy, and to protect President Donald Trump's ability to discreetly seek counsel.' (LEVINE. 2017)

◆◆◆◆◆◆◆

Trump will not release tax returns

'The White House response is that he's not going to release his tax returns," Conway said. "We litigated this all through the election. People didn't care," she said. "They voted for him, and let me make this very clear: Most Americans are very focused on what their tax returns will look like while President Trump is in office, not what his look like. And you know full well that President Trump and his family are complying with all the ethical rules, everything they need to do to step away from his businesses and be a full-time president."' (BRADNER. 2017)

◆◆◆◆◆◆◆

Why we march

'Now that Americans are getting into crunch time with filing their taxes, it's important to remember what's usually supposed to happen in early April. Around this same time of year, presidents customarily release their tax returns to the public. It's been a tradition for decades, but apparently that's not going to happen in 2017. Before Donald J. Trump was sworn into office, I authored legislation requiring all sitting presidents to release their tax returns, a practice that has been routine for every president since Watergate. It looks like Mr. Trump will choose to keep his returns secret and ignore this very low ethical bar, even though it's clear his "blind trust" isn't blind at all and the separation he promised he'd make from his businesses seems to be nonexistent.

Support for Mr. Trump to release his tax returns has only grown. It's stretched across both sides of the Capitol and has come from both sides of the aisle. Trump's tax returns have become a topic of conversation among more families, friends and communities. It's an issue that's been raised at each and every one of the 23 town halls I've hosted in Oregon this year. And as we approach tax day Americans across the country are turning up the pressure on Trump to release his returns.' (WYDEN. 2017)

◆◆◆◆◆◆◆

U.S. Image Plummets Under Trump White House, Pew Survey Says

'The drop in favorability ratings for the United States is widespread," Pew said. "The share of the public with a positive view of the U.S. has plummeted in a diverse set of countries from Latin America, North America, Europe, Asia and Africa. Favorability ratings have only increased in Russia and Vietnam."

The survey was conducted among 40,447 respondents in 37 countries from Feb. 16 to May 8. Asked about Trump's character, 75 percent said he's "arrogant," 65 percent said "ignorant," and 62 percent said "dangerous."' (VISCUSI. 2017)

◆◆◆◆◆◆◆

Chinese Media Can't Stop Making Fun Of Donald Trump

'Trump slaps self in face, again." Chinese media has referred to Trump's election a "democracy malfunction," compared him to Benito Mussolini and Adolf Hitler, called him "as ignorant as a child" and mocked his spelling problems. During the presidential campaign, media in the country called Trump "big-mouthed" and "abusively forthright," and even compared him to a clown.' (MAZZA. 2017)

Does it matter that leaders around the world have a low opinion of Donald? After all, he campaigned on Making America Great Again – not making countries outside America great again.

Yes, it does actually. In this world of global cyber attacks and mounting terrorism, every country needs allies. Turning existing allies against America is a very dangerous and short sighted ploy.

As a leader, your reputation and your credibility are actually all you have. Reputations can take years to build and seconds to destroy. Credibility is always about building trust, if your followers start to doubt your word then pretty soon they will no longer be followers.

When things get to this stage for a leader, they actually only have three choices:

12. Accept that they have been an idiot and do whatever they need to do to change.

13. Grab everything they can while they wait for the axe to fall.

14. Fall on their sword: call it a day: hand in their notice.

Every leader needs to be 100% aware that they have absolutely no-one else to blame if they now find themselves in such a situation.

They haven't listened nor cared. They have been too full of their own self importance, and they've been found seriously wanting.

'Our Founding Fathers would shudder to see how easily forces outside the mainstream now seem to effortlessly push some senate leaders toward conduct people don't want from their elected leaders: abusing power; jumping through hoops to ingratiate themselves to the party base while step by step, day by day, real problems that keep American families up at night fall by the wayside here in Washington.'

John Kerry

Lesson 25: Make sure your information comes from reliable sources

Seth Meyers Tears Into Donald Trump's 'Crazy' Tweets During James Comey Hearing

'Witnesses in a hearing are fact-checking the president's tweets about that hearing during a hearing." Meyers went on to say: "All of this, of course, raises the question once again of where the president gets his information," said Meyers, suggesting that "we are now at the point where the crazy things the president says are making their way into the halls of Congress, and wasting the time of allies, intelligence officials and the FBI director.' (MORAN. 2017)

◆◆◆◆◆◆◆

Trump has nothing but contempt for facts and reality-based policy. Now it's backfiring.

'The administration has regularly shown contempt for the very idea that consequential policy decisions require serious justification or a weighing of their consequences. What's more, the Times report notes that those deeply consequential decisions — the rollback of climate policies, and the Trump budget's deep cuts to health and scientific research and to the Environmental Protection Agency — were done without input from administration scientists. Those actions have been taken without advice or guidance from scientists and engineers inside the White House. The few remaining policy advisers have ceased distributing daily memos on policy issues like climate change, machine-learning regulation, or the ethics of big data collection.' (SARGENT. 2017)

◆◆◆◆◆◆◆

Trump trusts Fox 'Fox & Friends' Over His Own Intelligence Community

'President Donald Trump on Monday touted a "Fox & Friends" report that the previous administration spied on him during the election — an idea that has been widely debunked. As Trump congratulated "Fox & Friends" on its "amazing reporting," he was ignoring analysis from his own intelligence officials that there's no evidence such surveillance occurred.' (SATLIN. 2017)

If your information is incorrect then basing your decisions on that information can only lead to disaster. Get as much information as you can on anything you need to make a decision about – it just makes common sense. You may not like what you learn; then that is tough – it still requires a leader to make rational decisions based on solid information and due diligence.

"A wise man gets more use from his enemies
than a fool from his friends."

Baltasar Gracián,

The Art of Worldly Wisdom

Lesson 26: Don't deny, denigrate, dismiss or debunk expert advice

Trump puts the planet on a dangerous path

'Under President Barack Obama's leadership, the world finally began addressing one of the greatest challenges human beings have ever faced, a multi-generational struggle to keep the planet temperate and accommodating to human life. President Trump's move to rip up Mr. Obama's climate policies are beyond reckless. Children studying his presidency will ask, "How could anyone have done this?

Climate science is complicated, but the basics are easy enough for those school-children to understand. When humans burn fossil fuels, they emit heat-trapping gases into the atmosphere. Releasing vast amounts of these gases for decades changes the atmosphere's chemistry, creating an ever-thicker blanket. The world has therefore warmed and will continue to warm; the more fossil fuel burned, the hotter the planet will get.

The human species still has time at least to moderate the trajectory. But on the course Mr. Trump set Tuesday, the prospect will be for sharp environmental disruption. Among many other things, scientists have predicted more and more intense heat waves, more volatile weather, more abrupt changes in the landscape, more destruction from invasive pests, more illness from microbes flourishing in warmer fresh water and more urban flooding. Americans alive today will saddle future generations with the costs of acting too late, when addressing the issue sooner would have been cheaper and far less destructive.' (EDITORIAL. 2017)

Trump has nothing but contempt for facts and reality-based policy. Now it's backfiring.

'The administration has regularly shown contempt for the very idea that consequential policy decisions require serious justification or a weighing of their consequences. What's more, the Times report notes that those deeply consequential decisions — the rollback of climate policies, and the Trump budget's deep cuts to health and scientific research and to the Environmental Protection Agency — were done without input from administration scientists. Those actions have been taken without advice or guidance from scientists and engineers inside the White House. The few remaining policy advisers have ceased distributing daily memos on policy issues like climate change, machine-learning regulation, or the ethics of big data collection.' (SARGENT. 2017)

◆◆◆◆◆◆◆

On climate change, Scott Pruitt causes an uproar — and contradicts the EPA's own website

'Scott Pruitt, the nation's top environmental official, strongly rejected the established science of climate change on Thursday, outraging scientists, environmentalists, and even his immediate predecessor at the Environmental Protection Agency. "I think that measuring with precision human activity on the climate is something very challenging to do and there's tremendous disagreement about the degree of impact, so no, I would not agree that it's a primary contributor to the global warming that we see," Pruitt, the newly installed EPA administrator, said on the CNBC program "Squawk Box."' (DENNIS. 2017)

———————————

S adly Trump's 'I-know-better-than-you' attitude seems to pervade most topics. In his mind, he is the world expert on pretty much everything.

In this case, he takes his 'know it all' attitude to a whole new level of incompetence and the generations ahead who will be the ones who 'pay' for his ignorance, will be very unforgiving.

So as leaders – get your facts straight before you shoot your mouth off about something you know little or nothing about or worse, something you care little about.

"If a man will begin with certainties, he shall end in doubts; but if he will be content to begin with doubts, he shall end in certainties."
Francis Bacon, The Advancement Of Learning

Lesson 27: Never ignore, rubbish or repudiate empirical research and data

Donald Trump & EPA Nominee Scott Pruitt Love Asbestos, Despite the Deadly Facts

'Fact: asbestos is an extremely toxic substance. Between 12,000-15,000 Americans die every year every year from asbestos-related diseases. The World Health Organization (WHO) lists asbestos as a Type I carcinogen (without a doubt carcinogenic), while the Environmental Protection Agency (EPA) repeatedly states "There is no known safe level of asbestos exposure." Over 100 years of scientific research has proven again and again, through countless studies, the undeniable truth: asbestos is a silent killer. Because of all of the irrefutable evidence of asbestos's deadliness, 58 countries worldwide have banned the toxic mineral outright. This makes sense, right? Well, not according to President Donald Trump'.' (SOKOLOVELAW. 2017)

♦♦♦♦♦♦♦

Donald Thinks Asbestos Fears Are a Mob Conspiracy

"'I believe that the movement against asbestos was led by the mob, because it was often mob-related companies that would do the asbestos removal. Great pressure was put on politicians, and as usual, the politicians relented. Millions of truckloads of this incredible fire-proofing material were taken to special "dump sites" and asbestos was replaced by materials that were supposedly safe but couldn't hold a candle to asbestos in limiting the ravages of fire."' (SIMONES. 2016)

♦♦♦♦♦♦♦

Asbestos and the dangers of a Trump Presidency

'The medical and scientific evidence supporting the dangers of asbestos is clear. There is no conspiracy, no desire to make real estate developers like Trump pay more simply out of spite. Asbestos kills, and claiming that such deaths are false and part of a mafia conspiracy ignores all of the pain and suffering that real people feel every day due to this dangerous substance.

The reality: Mesothelioma Cancer. Mesothelioma is a rare, aggressive form of cancer that primarily develops in the lining of the lungs (pleural mesothelioma) or the abdomen (peritoneal mesothelioma). Caused by asbestos, mesothelioma has no known cure and has a poor prognosis.' (STAFF. 2016)

In the Tom Hanks movie Forest Gump there is a classic line, "Stupid is, as stupid does." And as a leader nothing will shoot your credibility down faster than denying or dismissing empirical evidence backed by solid science, research or analysis.

However you cross the threshold from perhaps ignorant to just plain stupid when you begin to assert that any such evidence backed research is made up, lies or some part of an elaborate conspiracy.

In the case of asbestosis, the science is absolute and undeniable. It is a slow, painful and hideous killer and for any leader to dismiss this reality is totally irresponsible.

My recommendation to any leader who is unsure about their 'experts' advice is to simply get out of the tower, go visit and talk to the people most affected or impacted and witness the condition for themselves.

As a result, even if you have to back down and accept the reality of the research, the fact that you went and saw enables you to retract without looking foolish.

'Nothing is more dangerous than a dogmatic worldview.
Nothing more constraining, more blinding to innovation,
more destructive of openness to novelty.'
Stephen Jay Gould

Lesson 28: No leader can ever consider themselves above the law

Trump Staff 'Purging' Devices, Avoid Giving Possible Russia Evidence

'The investigation into any possible collusion between Trump's people and Russia is currently in progress. Because of this, various Trump staffers are said to be 'purging' their phones. These include staff serving the White House at present and those who worked in the Trump transition team. At the same time, they are also reportedly deleting various important information.' (ONG. 2107)

◆◆◆◆◆◆◆

Trump says he can't be sued for violence at his rallies because he won the election

'Throughout the 2016 presidential campaign, Trump and/or the Trump Campaign repeatedly urged people attending Trump political rallies to remove individuals who were voicing opposition," reads Bamberger's filing, which asks that Trump be forced to pay his damages, if he's found liable.' (SELK. 2017)

Writing and sending bizarre tweets at ungodly hours is one thing; trying to wipe electronic devices surely crosses a line.

Pride comes before the fall and sadly sooner or later, arrogance, ego, and the delusional belief that you can outsmart any and everyone will be a leader's downfall. The jails of the world are full of people who thought they were smarter than the law.

The tragedy is the positive results they could have achieved if they had just put a fraction of their energy into things that were legal and above board as opposed to getting caught up in some quick money making scheme or under the table deal.

If leaders do nothing else but figure out their 'value' system, then they will be doing themselves and their people the very best of favors. If the leader is clear on the lines they will not cross in business to make a dollar and the things they won't do no matter how much is on the table then the whole organization will be clear on that.

If we don't clarify and live our values, if we don't see them as absolute and non-negotiable, then when temptation comes knocking on our door (and it will), we leave ourselves open to getting caught up in all sorts of unsavory situations. And sadly, once you give in to temptation it has the potential to become as addictive as heroin.

"When honor and the law no longer stand on the same side of the line,
how do we choose?"

Anne Bishop, Heir to the Shadows

Lesson 29: Resist self-praise; avoid the 'hero syndrome' and never award yourself saint status

Trump compares himself to Lincoln. But Lincoln warned us about demagogues like him.

'In 1838, a 28-year-old Lincoln gave a talk to the Young Men's Lyceum of Spring-field, Illinois on "The Perpetuation of Our Political Institutions." Although it's one of his earliest published speeches, its prescience and timeliness make it a must read today. Lincoln was trying to imagine what danger or threat could destroy this great nation—and "by what means shall we fortify against it." Lincoln went on to say "Distinction will be his paramount object, and [with] nothing left to be done in the way of building up, he would set boldly to the task of pulling down."' (ROMM. 2017)

◆◆◆◆◆◆◆

Trump defends claims he predicted a lot of things

'When questioned about a litany of controversial statements -- from unrest in Sweden, to Brexit, to dues owed by NATO states -- Trump told Time magazine in an interview published Thursday that he often foresaw things that later were revealed to be true. "I'm a very instinctual person, but my instinct turns out to be right," he said. "I predicted a lot of things, some things that came to you a little bit later."' (MSN News. 2017)

◆◆◆◆◆◆◆

Praise for the chief: Trump's Cabinet tells him it's an 'honor' and 'blessing' to serve

'At today's Cabinet meeting — the first President Trump had held with everyone on board — White House Chief of Staff Reince Priebus spoke up to thank Trump "for the opportunity and blessing that you've given us to serve your agenda and the American people."

Priebus said he was offering words on behalf of everyone in the room. But one by one, pretty much everyone else seated around the table took the opportunity to lavish their leader with praise, too, as the media looked on.' (WAGNER. 2017)

NO! There is very little Donald has done that has impressed me, but when I read about this round-table fawning, I felt this administration had hit the bottom of the barrel. If this had been North Korea I wouldn't have been surprised; if it had taken place in the Kremlin, I wouldn't have batted an eyelid. But in the Whitehouse, people groveling to the leader!

Any leader worth their salt would have stopped this process in its tracks and possibly even reversed the conversation. Any normal leader would have been truly embarrassed by this activity; at best they would have said 'thanks, now let's move on to the agenda' or Trump could have turned things around and said 'let me tell each of you what it is that I value about YOU.'

Understand the 'Hero' Syndrome.

I've witnessed many owners and managers over the years trying to be what can best be called 'the hero.' They thrive on 'saving' their people.

This can look great – it makes our people feel loved and cared for. But it is one of those scenarios that causes me discomfort. Of course, if it happens once, and is genuine, then all hail the leader, it tells me that this person really cares about their people. But if it happens again and again, then something isn't right.

An example: I watched as the Republicans wrestled with the healthcare challenge. Trump and the Republicans had campaigned long and hard on repealing and replacing Obamacare – and then we had the big press announcement that the deal was 'done' and the Republicans now had the new healthcare bill sorted.

House Republicans pass bill to replace and repeal Obamacare

'In a major victory for President Donald Trump, the House has voted to dismantle the pillars of the Affordable Care Act and make sweeping changes to the nation's health care system.' (LEE. 2017)

Then low and behold Donald cut across their boughs and said the bill was 'mean.'

Trump calls House health care bill 'mean'

'President Donald Trump told Republican senators lunching at the White House Tuesday the house-passed health care reform bill he celebrated earlier this year was "mean."' (MERICA et al. 2017)

So what was that all about?

That's when I came to the realization that, I think Donald needs to be a hero to the people who voted him in. It says to them 'I'm looking after you. You can trust me.' According to Laura Berman Fortgang, the problem with setting up a 'hero' scenario is this:

Getting Off-Course: The Hero Syndrome

'What is the "Hero Syndrome"? It is an unconscious need to be needed, appreciated or valued that disguises itself as a good thing, but threatens to make you bitter and to overextend you. This insidious need will get met when you say yes and overpromise what you can deliver in order to be liked, please other people, or avoid the perceived consequences of saying no.

She goes on to say: The key to turning around the hero syndrome is understanding its source: needs. The hero is driven by the need for approval, recognition, and/or feeling needed and valued. The need is met briefly by the "high" of being asked to do something, but it is exactly this short-lived high that makes it an addictive cycle. In order to get it met, you have to keep saying yes.' (FORTGANG. 2012)

Don't fall into the hero trap; people don't actually need heroes they need leaders.

And in order to satisfy your hero fix, don't make yourself look good by expecting people to fawn over you and never betray the people who are trying to do your bidding. This massively demotivates people. Don't keep vacillating. Don't blow your own trumpet, learn the skills of humility and modesty. No-one likes a big noter. And never award yourself 'saint' status; it looks so bad and will actually come back to haunt you

Above all else, don't set something up and then sabotage it so you can ride in on your white charger to rescue the situation again. That is borderline loopy.

Was Lincoln prescient?

"A teachable spirit and a humbleness to admit your ignorance
or your mistake will save you a lot of pain.
However, if you're a person who knows it all, then you've got
a lot of heavy-hearted experiences coming your way."

Ron Carpenter Jr

Lesson 30: Avoid getting sucked into playing Blame Games!

Trump Blames Obamacare Defeat On Democrats Whom He Never Asked For Help

'In the moments after it was announced that his health care bill was dead and pulled from consideration, President Donald Trump had pinpointed the culprit. Democrats, he explained, were to blame for the failure because they refused to provide him with any of their votes.

"We had no Democrat support. We had no votes from the Democrats," Trump explained. "With no Democrats on board, we couldn't quite get there. When you get no votes from the other side — meaning the Democrats — it is a very difficult situation.' (STEIN. 2017)

◆◆◆◆◆◆◆

Trump blames McConnell for Senate crash of Obama health repeal

(FRAM. 2017)

For me, among the worst of all the terrible 'Trump' traits, is his need to always find someone to blame; the worker. Think about the determination to repeal and replace Obamacare. Why would the Democrats help Trump crash and burn the very thing they fought so hard to introduce? Why would they lift a finger after he had trashed their candidate at every opportunity? He had trashed and continues to trash then President Obama; he trashed their campaign; promised to put Clinton in jail etc.

And he thought they were going to bend over backward to help him?

You do have to wonder what goes on in Donald's head. And he didn't even ask. Though even if he had asked, I doubt the outcome would have been any different. Again, why would they lift a finger?

And it isn't just the Democrats he has blamed:

- He blamed [i]Melania's speech writer for copying Michelle Obama's speech.
- He blamed [ii]President Obama for the protests.
- He blames [iii]the press for everything.
- He blamed [iv]a judge for his own ill-conceived travel ban.
- He blames [v]Obama for the Russian hacking.

- He blamed the FBI director for the firing of James Comey.
- He blames McConnell for the failure to repeal and replace Obamacare.

> **Donald J. Trump** ✔
> @realDonaldTrump
>
> **I am being investigated for firing the FBI Director by the man who told me to fire the FBI Director! Witch Hunt**
>
> 6:07 AM - 16 Jun 2017

There are a few very simple rules around the dangers of the blame game:

- It makes the blamer look really sad and pathetic.
- It diminishes the respect your followers have for you.
- It suggests the leader doesn't have the courage to look in the mirror As leaders, we don't have to be able to walk on water. It's ok to say 'I messed up, I was found wanting I will learn from this, and I will never do it again.'

So if you want help – ask. If you need help – let people know. But, don't expect help from people you have trashed... EVER!

A leader is someone who has no difficulty is asking themselves, 'how did I set this up?'

If you are the leader - then the buck has to stop with you.

> "'At the end of the day, you are solely responsible for your success and your failure. And the sooner you realize that, you accept that, and integrate that into your work ethic, you will start being successful. As long as you blame others for the reason you aren't where you want to be, you will always be a failure."
>
> Erin Cummings

---

i. Michelle Broder Van Dyke, BuzzFeed 19/7/2016. Melania Trump Copied Part of Her Speech From Michelle Obama

ii. Jennifer Epstein, Stuff 1/3/2017. Donald Trump blames Barack Obama for protests I think he's behind it. http://www.stuff.co.nz/world/americas/89913893/Donald-Trump-blames-Barack-Obama-for-protests-I-think-hes-behind-it

iii. Jeremy Diamond, CNN 1/6/2016. Trump launches all-out attack on press. http://edition.cnn.com/2016/05/31/politics/donald-trump-veterans-announcement/index.html

iv. Don Melvin, Ali Arouzi and Shamar Walters, NBC News 4/2/2017. Homeland Security Suspends Implementation of President Trump's Travel Ban. http://www.nbcnews.com/news/us-news/judge-halts-trump-travel-ban-banned-countries-citizens-able-board-n716801

v. Sam Levine, Huffpost 22/6/2017. Trump Isn't Sure If Russian Hacking Happened, But Is Still Blaming

Lesson 31: Don't make promises you have no hope of keeping (and shouldn't have made in the first place)

PROMISE NUMBER 1: DRAIN THE SWAMP

How Trump Plans to Drain the Swamp

'One of Donald Trump's central presidential campaign promises was to "drain the swamp" by ridding Washington politics of corruption and corporate influence. Here's how he plans to do it.

Say it a lot.

Fill cabinet with Wall Street executives to ensure as many billionaires as possible are incriminated in any potential impeachment proceedings.

Cancel Easter Egg Roll.

Cut funding for the cesspool of nepotism and greed known as the National Science Foundation.

Getting Rick Perry involved should do the trick.

Tax cuts for high earners so that CEOs are no longer forced to make ends meet by taking jobs in presidential administration.

End illegal Washington corruption by legalizing it.

Lose 2020 reelection'   (THE ONION. 2017)

♦♦♦♦♦♦♦

Will 'drain the swamp' be Trump's first broken promise?

'In the final stretch of his campaign, Donald Trump made "drain the swamp" a catch-all slogan for everything his supporters despised about Washington: lobbyists, corruption, campaign finance and pay-to-play. But in the weeks since Election Day, Trump and his allies have engaged in some of the same practices they accused Hillary Clinton of exploiting and vowed to change: cashing in on government connections by opening lobbying firms; enabling people to enrich themselves from government service; and selling access to the president-elect and his family.' (ARNSDORF et al. 2016)

◆◆◆◆◆◆◆

'Day 138. There are two things on Trump's agenda today. The first is to sign an executive order that will repeal a regulation that was designed to keep shady contractors from benefiting from tax dollars. The rule said that companies with an egregious record of violating wage and safety laws would lose their government contracts if they didn't come into compliance. What that means is that if a contractor stole wages through shady payroll practices, or had too many safety violations, they could lose their contract. But, Republicans said t was too punitive and a "job killer". Yeah, everyone wants to work for a contractor that does not adhere to safety rules and is willing to steal their workers pay for themselves.' (LEAN LEFT. 2017)

◆◆◆◆◆◆◆

PROMISE NUMBER 2: BRING BACK JOBS

Trump promised to bring back coal jobs.

'Industry experts say coal mining jobs will continue to be lost, not because of blocked access to coal, but because power plant owners are turning to natural gas. At least six plants that relied on coal have closed or announced they will close since Trump's victory in November, including the main plant at the Navajo Generating Station in Arizona, the largest in the West. Another 40 are projected to close during the president's four-year term.' (FEARS. 2017)

◆◆◆◆◆◆◆

PROMISE NUMBER 3: BUILD THAT WALL

Can Trump's wall be built? Will it be effective? Should you bid? No, no and no. Here's why.

'Early cost estimates for the 1,300 mile long wall run around $38 billion—the single most expensive infrastructure project ever undertaken in the U.S. The CBP says it will announce finalists in June.' (JACKSON. 2017)

Every leader wants to make their mark; hopefully for the right reasons; hopefully, it's because they want to make improvements and add value to their followers. It just makes sense to analyze why you want to make the changes. Analyze also the costs vs. the benefits.

- Draining the swamp was a great election slogan, the reality is that Trump seems to be building a deeper and radically more expensive and out of touch swamp.

- Bringing back jobs in the oil and coal sector is so far out of step with virtually every other nation on earth with regard to climate change, that it beggars belief as to why Trump is even doing this. No-one can bring jobs back when the technology for doing those jobs has moved on. The double whammy here is that even if these jobs could be brought back, removing safety checks on what is probably one of the most dangerous jobs in the world is totally irresponsible.

- The wall – not only did he promise to build it he promised faithfully that Mexico would pay for it; which is highly unlikely. As [i]Pope Francis said – 'instead of building a wall, build a bridge!'

He is making promises to people that he simply can't keep. Imagine if, instead of saying 'I will bring your jobs back,' he could have said:

'It is really sad that these jobs are no longer viable, sadly technology and the world have moved on. So my promise to you is that we will instigate training programs for people who have lost jobs to technology, so you can retrain in another field where jobs are plentiful.' Or words to that effect.

Now that would be leadership.

"All of the things that you promised me that you'd be, now your hands are tied. And all of the things that you promised me that you'd need, now my hands are tied."

Tegan Quin

i. Telegraph Video, The Telegraph 8/2/2017. Pope denounces Donald Trump saying build bridges not walls. http://www.telegraph.co.uk/news/2017/02/08/pope-denounces-donald-trump-saying-build-bridges-not-walls/

Lesson 32: Leaders look forward, losers look back

Trump puts the planet on a dangerous path

"Under President Barack Obama's leadership, the world finally began addressing one of the greatest challenges human beings have ever faced, a multi-generational struggle to keep the planet temperate and accommodating to human life. President Trump's move to rip up Mr. Obama's climate policies are beyond reckless. Children studying his presidency will ask, "How could anyone have done this?"

Climate science is complicated, but the basics are easy enough for those school-children to understand. When humans burn fossil fuels, they emit heat-trapping gases into the atmosphere. Releasing vast amounts of these gases for decades changes the atmosphere's chemistry, creating an ever-thicker blanket. The world has therefore warmed and will continue to warm; the more fossil fuel burned, the hotter the planet will get.

The human species still has time at least to moderate the trajectory. But on the course Mr. Trump set Tuesday, the prospect will be for sharp environmental disruption. Among many other things, scientists have predicted more and more intense heat waves, more volatile weather, more abrupt changes in the landscape, more destruction from invasive pests, more illness from microbes flourishing in warmer fresh water and more urban flooding. Americans alive today will saddle future generations with the costs of acting too late, when addressing the issue sooner would have been cheaper and far less destructive.' (EDITORIAL. 2017)

Messages about climate change have been shouted from the rooftops for many years now. We keep being told by scientists that time is running out for us to do something about it. We are witnessing weather events previously only witnessed once every hundred and even thousand years.

If anyone still doubts that we have a man-made problem, then all they need to do is look at the air pollution in China, the bleaching of The Great Barrier Reef and the recent hurricanes Harvey and Irma.

Let's not delude ourselves, climate change is real. And time really is running out.

Air pollution in China

Aftermath of Hurricane Irma

Bleached Coral Australia

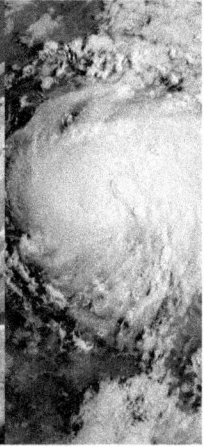

Satellite image of Hurricane Harvey

'Every human has four endowments: self awareness, conscience, independent will and creative imagination. These give us the ultimate human freedom. The power to choose, to respond to change.'

Unknown -

Lesson 33: If you don't show leadership rest assured, someone else will

Donald Trump withdraws US from Paris climate deal

'The 2015 accord united most of the world in a single agreement to mitigate climate change for the first time. It was signed by 195 countries out of 197 in a UN group on climate change, with Syria and Nicaragua abstaining.

US allies voiced dismay over Mr Trump's move, and France, Germany and Italy dismissed his suggestion that the global pact could be revised. French president Emmanuel Macron categorically ruled out any renegotiation and said Mr Trump's decision would harm American interests and citizens.' (BBC. 2017)

◆◆◆◆◆◆◆

The future leaves clues

'ENERGY DISRUPTION. This week, California ISO, a California electric company, announced it hit an all-time peak served by renewables of 56.7 percent (electricity).

California is on track to meet its 50 percent clean energy target by 2030 with ease. What it Means. We're heading towards a wholesale change in the energy economy over the next 20 years. From hydrocarbon (oil, gas, coal) to all electric, think massive-solar.

I used to think that gas-guzzling cars would maintain the petrochemical industry for a few more decades, but electric-autonomous "car as a service" will cause us each to park, sell, or junk our internal-combustion cars for something that is 10x cheaper and much better (i.e. autonomous Ubers).

Get ready for oil and gas to go the way of whale oil. Once useful, eventually laughable. Remember that energy is not scarce.

We have 8,000 times more energy hitting the Earth's surface in one day than we consume as an entire species. That energy, the solar flux, isn't yet in a easily usable form.

But that is changing... fast.

Given the global, exponential growth in solar and the coming innovations in battery technologies (I get five to 10 introductions to new battery technology companies each month), plus deployments like Tesla's Gigafactory, I'm firmly convinced we're heading towards a transition.

Coal is already dead.

Oil and gas may not be far behind.' (DIAMANDIS. 2017)

I f ever we needed courageous leadership in the world, it is right now. Climate change is the single biggest issue for this planet... that is if we actually want the next generations to have somewhere to live.

How any leader can't see that; doesn't want to see that; or in Trump's case actively negates what 197 countries have finally agreed on, actually beggars' belief. [i]The only 2 countries that have NOT signed the Paris agreement are Syria; which to be fair seems buried in a never ending civil war and Nicaragua. Nicaragua refused to sign not because they didn't agree with the targets, but because they felt the targets weren't strict enough.

Even North Korea signed.

Why would a leader not want to see their people with clean air and clean water? Why would they want to witness floods and cyclones wiping out whole communities because of their inaction?

'Saving our planet, lifting people out of poverty,
advancing economic growth... these are one and the same fight.
We must connect the dots between climate change,
water scarcity, energy shortages, global health,
food security and women's empowerment.
Solutions to one problem must be solutions for all.'

Ban Ki-moon

---

i. Alexander C. Kaufman, Huffpost 5/3/2017 - Only 2 countries aren't part of the Paris agreement. Will the U.S. be the third? http://www.huffingtonpost.com/entry/countries-not-in-paris-agreement_us_5909ee4ce4b02655f842f072

Lesson 34: Don't bully people; don't let your people bully people and don't undercut your people

Steve Bannon Thought He Could Bully Republicans On Health Care. He Couldn't.

'Bannon reportedly said. "This is not a discussion. This is not a debate. You have no choice but to vote for this bill." Bannon apparently did not count on the fact that House Republicans knew they actually did have a choice in the matter.

"You know, the last time someone ordered me to something, I was 18 years old," one of the members reportedly told Bannon. "And it was my daddy. And I didn't listen to him, either."' (MURDOCH. 2017)

◆◆◆◆◆◆◆

Move fast and break things: Trump's Obamacare failure and the backlash ahead

'That policy too was imposed with a missionary zeal that masked a lack of competence and grasp of detail. But Trump appears to be playing the role of a chief executive intent on shaking up a business and his chief strategist.' (SMITH. 2017)

◆◆◆◆◆◆◆

Trump Undercuts his Aids By Contradicting Their Statements

'Members of President Trump's Cabinet and top White House aides tried to soften his travel ban by calling it a "temporary pause." They said his firing of former FBI director James B. Comey was not about the Russia investigation. And this week they used their public comments to attempt to keep the United States out of a messy regional conflict in the Middle East.

But every time, Trump weighed in with a different message that effectively undercut what his aides and Cabinet secretaries appeared to be trying to achieve.

Trump's aides are quickly learning they speak for the president at their own peril.' (PHILLIPS. 2017)

Don't make your staff look foolish by publicly contradicting what they say; don't confuse 'assertiveness' with 'abuse' and don't confuse 'negotiating' with 'bullying.' Negotiating suggests a win/win. Bullying may get you a win (this time), but there will be a cost. Sooner or later you will find no-one wants to work for you. Then what?

The movers and shakers in your team, those who bought into the vision and mission because they believed in it, and you, will take offense and leave. And you're not so assertive people will stay. But the people who stay will now be working under a cloud of fear which will affect their health; diminish their productivity, and they will cease thinking for themselves out of fear.

When I hear managers or team leaders say 'my people seem unable to think for themselves' I wonder – is that because you don't let them?

Leaders need to realize the power they hold over people; abusing that power is not ok.

"I would rather be a little nobody,
then to be an evil somebody."
Abraham Lincoln

Lesson 35: Be professional at all times

Donald Trump mocked for 'awkward' handshake with Japanese Prime Minister Shinzo Abe

'The President of these United States of America met with the Prime Minister of Japan on Friday. They discussed some stuff. Then, they shook hands. And that's when things just got kind of objectively weird.' (STRACHAN. 2017)

But then the 'handshake' issue got worse:

♦♦♦♦♦♦♦

Donald refuses to shake Angela Merkel's hand

'Mrs Merkel grimaced slightly but soon brushed off the awkward incident and began the task of attempting to build a new transatlantic partnership, quipping in their later press conference that the two leaders "will work together hand in hand.' (ROTHWELL. 2017)

And then he met President Macron!

Emmanuel Macron proves why the Trump handshake matters so much

'The newly elected French president told a French journal on Sunday that his handshake with US President Donald Trump during a meeting during the NATO gathering in Brussels last week was about much more than just an exchange of pleasantries.

"My handshake with him, it's not innocent," Macron said. "It's not the alpha and the omega of politics, but a moment of truth."

He added: "One must show that we won't make little concessions, even symbolic ones."

And so Donald's hand-shake humiliation game with other world leaders seriously backfired when Macron gave it right back at him.

And the whole world was watching.' (CILLIZZA. 2017)

Incidents like these really are bizarre. Clearly, Trump loves publicity; he loves being the center of attention, but the reality was that his game of 'pat the puppy' with Prime Minister Abe and flat refusal to shake the hand of Mrs. Merkle were clearly humiliating to both foreign leaders. He made a mockery of diplomacy and he showed the world stage exactly who he is.

No matter what his thoughts are in private about Mrs. Merkle – she is The Chancellor of Germany. She is a former research scientist with a doctorate in physical chemistry. She came to the USA to discuss not only trade issues but also the future of NATO.

However such behavior never goes unpunished and as every school yard bully eventually discovers, you will meet your match... and in watching the video of Trumps attempt to dominate President Macron with a handshake at the NATO gathering in Brussels (May, 2017), it's clear that Trump lost that encounter; as young people would say, "Trump got owned!"

Regardless of this however, such behavior from a head of state or any leader is singularly unprofessional.

So as a leader, remember you really are on your own 'stage'; you must be professional at all times.

'Blowing out someone else's candle
doesn't make yours shine any brighter'
Not Known

Chapter 6

Beware conflicts of interest at all times

"No matter their party,
people with a conflict of interest
should be banned from the
Electoral College."

- DaShanne Stokes -

Lesson 36: There is no right way to do a wrong thing: learn from the mistakes of the past

Donald Trump's conflicts of interest continue as sons attend policy meetings while running his businesses

'On Tuesday, Trump said his sons would run his company, building what he says is a clear wall between his private business and public power. On Wednesday, his children had seats at the table of one of his biggest policy meetings yet, attended by the country's top tech-industry elites and Trump Cabinet nominees. Also around the table: bottles of Trump Natural Spring Water, the president-elect's water brand.' (HARWELL. 2016)

A leader must be above shady transactions at all times. It may be tempting to do a few under-the-table deals that make a quick return and that you are sure no-one will ever find out about, but they will find out. Truth always comes out in the end. And then what?

Trust and reputation go hand in hand, if you are not trustworthy, then your reputation will be shot, sooner or later.

Usually 'sooner.'

"We often hear of someone saying, 'So you don't trust me' or 'Are you questioning my integrity?' or 'You don't believe me.' They get defensive and angry because someone questions their actions, and they think they are above being questioned or having to prove their trustworthiness. But none of us is above questioning."

Henry Cloud

Lesson 37: Never let the lure of money lead you into murky waters

A scramble to assess the dangers of President-elect Donald Trump's global business empire

'Donald Trump's company has been paid up to $10 million by the tower's developers since 2014 to affix the Trump name atop the luxury complex, whose owner, one of Turkey's biggest oil and media conglomerates, has become an influential megaphone for the country's increasingly repressive regime. That, ethics advisers said, forces the Trump complex into an unprecedented nexus: as both a potential channel for dealmakers seeking to curry favor with the Trump White House and a potential target for attacks or security risks overseas. The president-elect's Turkey deal marks a harrowing vulnerability that even Trump has deemed "a little conflict of interest": a private money-maker that could open him to foreign influence and tilt his decision-making as America's executive in chief. Some companies reflect long-established deals while others were launched as recently as Trump's campaign, including eight that appear tied to a potential hotel project in Saudi Arabia, the oil-rich Arab kingdom that Trump has said he "would want to protect.' (HARWELL. 2016)

Be very clear what your role in a company (or country) is. If it is to look after the company's (or country's) interests – and it should have been – then feathering your own nest at the same time is distinctly shabby.

And how much money will ever be enough for Trump? What is his great 'emptiness' that requires him to look for more and more and more? It would be sad if it weren't so tragic for America and the people who voted for him. There will be a pay back of course.

At some stage, all the money in the world won't be enough to protect a leader from the mess they have single handily created in their quest for more and more and more.

'Would that there was an award for people who come to
understand the concept of enough. Good enough.
Successful enough. Thin enough. Rich enough.
When you have self-respect you have enough.'

Gail Sheehey

Chapter 7

Understand the nature of your team and how your skill set fits

'Individual commitment to a group effort
- that is what makes a team work,
a company work, a society work,
a civilization work.'

Vince Lombardi

Lesson 38: A leader must find ways to take ALL their people with them

How a secret Freedom Caucus pact brought down Obamacare repeal

'Freedom Caucus members told the White House they distrusted Ryan because he doesn't listen to their concerns. They refused to work with him, going around his back to negotiate with the White House. Little Trump did to woo them worked because the group always wanted more, White House officials and GOP leadership insiders said. They were buoyed by outside groups rooting them on, and didn't fear the White House's fury because the law was unpopular — and, increasingly, so was the president.' (BADE et al. 2017)

Building trust takes time, and so the larger the organization you are now leading, the more time it will take to gain buy-in from your people. You will need to meet and greet as often as it takes to communicate your plan or your goal; you will need to be very clear why you are doing what you are doing so you can articulate your vision but also deal with people who are not convinced.

A leader also needs to decide what to do about the 'recalcitrant's,' the people in his team who would take everything down because of their personal agendas.

In any team or organization, these people need to be dealt with in a way that leaves no doubt that they either come with you or they must leave. Not quite sure how that would work in American politics, but this is where a leader needs to be a good negotiator; to work WITH such people rather than against them.

A good leader will find workable compromises. And a great leader will be willing to look outside his team for supporters if that is what is required. Otherwise, these same people will prevent a leader achieving anything. The saboteurs will weaken your vision because you haven't involved them; you haven't listened to them, and you haven't sold it to them, OR you haven't removed them.

Did he investigate sufficiently across the various divisions to find out where people stood or did he just want some quick runs on the board after all the promises he had made during his election campaign? Or did he just want to be made to look 'good'?

In reality, the Republican Party had spent seven years belittling Obamacare and promising to repeal it, yet when they had the opportunity they had no plan; no blueprint ready and waiting, and they didn't even have the numbers. Why was that?

Did Trump think that all the ground work was done and it was just a case of implementing the change? Had he spent enough time with Paul Ryan, the man who was charged with repealing the legislation to really understand, a) the process, b) the likely success factors, c) the likely stumbling blocks?

Did Trump factor in that at this early stage of their relationship realize that he and Paul Ryan needed to work together to 'sell' the changes?

I read that Paul Ryan is a man who is passionate about policy and procedures but is not a salesman, while Trump is a salesman who is not interested in policy and procedures. Together they may have had a chance but by Trump leaving it to Paul Ryan and just waiting for a 'win' Trump imperiled the outcome just as much as Paul Ryan.

'My friend, you can't expect to unify overnight a country which boasts 257 different types of cheese.'

General de Gaulle

Lesson 39: Be careful whom you recruit; why you recruit them and the impression that gives

Donald Trump unaware Michael Flynn was a 'foreign agent'

'Flynn resigned in February after just four weeks as national security adviser when it came to light that he had misled the vice-president, Mike Pence about phone conversations with the Russian ambassador about sanctions in December. The resignation came after a flow of intelligence leaks revealed he had secretly discussed sanctions with the ambassador, Sergey Kislyak and then tried to cover up the conversations.' (JAMIESON. 2107)

We can all make recruitment mistakes. It isn't unusual to have people in an interview telling the interviewer what they want to hear. But Flynn was known to Trump; it wasn't as if they had never met.

[i]President Obama actually warned Trump not to employ him.

So did Trump really not know Flynn's background? I find it surprising that he didn't. And if he knowingly recruited someone with such credentials, what does that say about Trump himself.

So if in doubt (even when you think you know a person), in fact especially when you think you know a person:

- Check references
- Check references
- Check references

'Denial is not a river in Egypt'
Stuart Smalley

---

i. Julian Borger, The Guardian. 8/5/2017. https://www.theguardian.com/us-news/2017/may/08/obama-warned-trump-michael-flynn-russia-contacts

Addition Notes – Definition of transformational leadership:
Transformational leadership is a style of leadership where a leader works with subordinates to identify needed change, creating a vision to guide the change through inspiration, and executing the change in tandem with committed members of a group.[1] Transformational leadership serves to enhance the motivation, morale, and job performance of followers through a variety of mechanisms; these include connecting the follower's sense of identity and self to a project and to the collective identity of the organization; being a role model for followers in order to inspire them and to raise their interest in the project; challenging followers to take greater ownership for their work, and understanding the strengths and weaknesses of followers, allowing the leader to align followers with tasks that enhance their performance. (Source: Wikipedia)

Lesson 40: People don't join organizations. They join great leaders

President Trump Keeps Firing People Who Are Investigating President Trump

'Analysts and lawmakers say they are troubled by a trend in the president's firing decisions.

Former FBI Director James Comey, former U.S. Attorney Preet Bharara and former acting U.S. Attorney General Sally Yates were all fired by President Donald Trump while they investigated him.' (TOOMBS. 2017)

◆◆◆◆◆◆◆

Help Wanted. Why Republicans Won't work for Trump

'Republicans say they are turning down job offers to work for a chief executive whose volatile temperament makes them nervous. They are asking head-hunters if their reputations could suffer permanent damage, according to 27 people The Washington Post interviewed to assess what is becoming a debilitating factor in recruiting political appointees.' (REIN. 2017)

Anyone in leadership will tell you that their success depends on getting the right people around them. When a new leader is employed, there will quite naturally be some turnover of staff. Some people will have long term loyalty to the previous leader and feel it is time for them to move on. That is normal. However, mass dismissals and turnover in the early days of a new leader is not a good thing.

Having been an HR Manager and consultant for over 30 years, I can absolutely attest to the effects of high turnover:

- Morale is affected which in turn affects productivity.

- The loss of knowledge and experience can't be underestimated.

- The environment becomes fearful, which leads to stress and absenteeism.

- Fearful people don't make good decisions if they even have the confidence to make decisions at all.

- All innovation is stifled because over worked people are now endlessly trying to fill the holes left by the people who have gone elsewhere.

Look after your people, and they will look after you.

'When your forces are dulled your edge is blunted,
your strength is exhausted, and your supplies are gone,
then others will take advantage of your debility and rise up.
Then even if you have wise advisers,
you cannot make things turn out well in the end.'

Sun Tzu. The Art of War

Lesson 41: Remember your people have teams and agendas also

Trump tastes failure as U.S. House healthcare bill collapses

'President Donald Trump suffered a stunning political setback on Friday in a Congress controlled by his own party when Republican leaders pulled legislation to overhaul the U.S. healthcare system, a major 2016 election campaign promise of the president and his allies. At the other extreme 'uncertainty over a replacement and a Congressional Budget Office estimate that 24 million Americans could end up without health insurance mean that there may be a heavy price to pay for action which greatly concerned the house moderates. For the moderates these were the people who had voted them into office so they were not about to betray their voters!' (REUTERS. 2017)

◆◆◆◆◆◆◆

Rattled by CBO report, moderate Republicans turn against GOP bill

'"I plan to vote NO on the current #AHCA bill. As written the plan leaves too many from my #SoFla district uninsured," the Florida congresswoman wrote in two consecutive tweets. "As #AHCA stands, it will cut much needed help for #SoFla's poor + elderly populations. Need a plan that will do more to protect them."' (FOX. 2017)

◆◆◆◆◆◆◆

Republicans up for reelection who are taking part in the Trumpcare Kamikaze Mission will be voted out of office in the 2018

'History is about to repeat itself, only this time, it will be the Republicans who will suffer a bloodbath in the midterm elections next year.' (SHAN. 2017)

In any team, you will have a continuum of 'buy in.' Some of your team will be with you 100%; some not so clearly defined and others will resist whatever change you want to implement. Not because they are bad people, rather they have their own people and agendas.

In this case, it was the Freedom Caucus that collapsed the healthcare bill; people who were supposedly on the same wave-length as Trump, after all, they were Republicans. But they were on the outer edge of what Trump wanted, and in their view, he didn't take the bill far enough towards what they wanted.

So a 'team' in crisis even at this early stage of Trump's presidency.

But Trump's team conflict comes back to his own leadership. You can't rush change of this magnitude; you can't force people to vote just to make you, the leader, look good. You have to take time; you have to take people with you and if whatever change it is you want to implement, isn't ready or your people are not entirely behind it, then don't implement it.

Trump is a business man – he is used to telling someone to do something, and they do it – no questions asked. That isn't the way it's done now he is President – he has to manage a lot of differing agendas. He has to be hands-on at least in the early stages; he has to be willing to get his hands dirty. He had to get involved.

'No team is ever far from betrayal, from the outside and the inside, and this creates a tension few consider exquisite.
Teams are hard work, mentally and emotionally.'
Harvey Robbins and Michael Finley, Why Teams Don't Work

Lesson 42: Make sure you and your team sing from the same hymn sheet

Tillerson, defending Trump policy, contradicted by his words

'Tillerson and his agency have repeatedly appeared out of sync with comments from Trump and the White House on critical matters, at the risk of sowing confusion and anxiety among U.S. friends and foes.

The secretary's appearances Tuesday and Wednesday before House and Senate committees come days Tillerson and Trump issued divergent messages on the Qatar crisis received widespread attention. But that was only the latest example of conflicting messages.

Last month, Tillerson was overruled by the president after urging him not to withdraw from the Paris climate agreement. In his Senate confirmation hearing, Tillerson said he supported staying in, to preserve U.S. leverage on other countries. His former company, Exxon Mobil, also supported staying in the deal. When Trump chose to withdraw, Tillerson and the State Department remained quiet as other Cabinet agencies praised the decision.' (LEE. 2017)

When a leader and his/her senior team are discussing and deciding strategic policy, it is actually a no-brainer that all members are in agreement as to what the policy is and there is consensus on what policy statements are given out to the public.

Constant conflicting information coming from administrators and Trump make them all look totally inept. It suggests that either the Trump administration doesn't actually have key policies in place on major issues or that the policies change depending on Donald's mood that day.

A great way to humiliate your team and yourself on a global scale.

'The way a team plays as a whole determines its success.
You may have the best individual stars in the world,
but if they don't play together the club won't be worth a dime.'

Babe Ruth

Lesson 43: Don't put members of your family on your senior team

President Donald Trump gives daughter Ivanka White House office

'Donald Trump has increased his family's grip on the White House by installing his daughter Ivanka close to the Oval Office and giving her access to state secrets. An administration official confirmed reports that the President's 35-year-old daughter would be getting her own West Wing office, classified information clearance, and a government-issued phone.

The admission would have dismayed anti-nepotism campaigners, coming just two months after her husband Jared Kushner was given a senior position in the administration.

Since her father was elected, Ms Trump has raised conflict of interest questions by appearing at meetings with world leaders, including with Japan's Prime Minister Shinzo Abe in November. It was later revealed that the meeting came at the same time she was trying to negotiate a lucrative deal for her clothing line with a state-backed Japanese firm.' (TUBB. 2107)

The appointment of his daughter is wrong on so many levels. If you are a leader and you put one of your family members on your team, you immediately create an imbalance of power. You also create a trust issue because the rest of your team will always be afraid that whatever they say will be reported back to you, which is the absolute WORST way to build trust and respect in a team.

There will also be a credibility problem if your family member has no credentials to BE on the team.

It actually doesn't do any favors for your family member either – they know deep down that they got the job for all the wrong reasons.

'The original communitarianism of Chinese Confucian Society has degenerated into nepotism; a system of family linkages and corruption on the mainland. And remnants of the evils of the original system are still found in Taiwan, Hong Kong, and even Singapore.'
Lee Kuan Yew

Lesson 44: Be wary of putting inexperienced people into incredibly complex roles: set your people up for success

Trump taps Kushner to lead a swat team to fix government with business ideas

'In a White House riven at times by disorder and competing factions, the innovation office represents an expansion of Kushner's already far-reaching influence. The 36-year-old former real estate and media executive will continue to wear many hats, driving foreign and domestic policy as well as decisions on presidential personnel. He also is a shadow diplomat, serving as Trump's lead adviser on relations with China, Mexico, Canada and the Middle East.' (PARKER. 2017)

———————————

Kushner is, of course, Trump's son-in-law, married to his daughter Ivanka and he is also one of Trump's trusted advisers.

According to Wikipedia - Kushner is an American real estate investor and developer. But now, suddenly, he has responsibilities for driving American foreign and domestic policy while being an adviser on relations with China, Mexico (and that wall), Canada and the Middle East.

Really? Firstly, I have nothing wrong with any leader bringing in young people with fresh ideas and from different backgrounds; hopefully, new eyes will bring ideas and energy. However, the last thing a leader should do with such people is to give them portfolios which are way beyond their skills, experience, and abilities.

The Middle East? My goodness – what can Kushner do that so many dedicated people before him were unable to do? Talk about setting someone up for ridicule and abject failure. President Obama had eight years to work on the area, and even he said, 'there are no short cuts, no detours in the Middle East.'

But also let's discuss the rationale that leaders should set their people up for success because to me it seems that Trump is setting Kushner up for failure. There is no way this young man is equipped to do justice to even one of these portfolios – he simply doesn't have the background, gravitas, and/or experience; but let's be even more realistic here - no one could manage this number of duties; it is physically and humanly impossible.

> 'We can stay in Afghanistan and the Middle East forever,
> and it won't make a bit of difference.'

Virgil Goode

Lesson 45: Don't overload young managers: let them find their feet

White House Announces Jared Kushner Is Now Responsible For Everything

'Over the weekend, the president's philosophy on running the country suddenly became more clear. Trump wants to get a lot of work done, he just wants his son-in-law, Jared Kushner, to do it. Kushner has been tapped to run an entirely new office with the "sweeping authority to overhaul the federal bureaucracy and fulfill key campaign promises — such as reforming care for veterans and fighting opioid addiction. So, if you're keeping track, Jared Kushner, who comes to Washington with no government experience, no policy experience, no diplomatic experience, and business experience limited to his family's real estate development firm, a brief stint as a newspaper publisher, and briefly bidding to acquire the Los Angeles Dodgers, will be working on trade, Middle East policy in general, an Israel-Palestine peace deal more specifically, reforming the Veterans Administration, and solving the opioid crisis.

Apparently, this new office will also be responsible for "modernizing the technology and data infrastructure of every federal department and agency; remodeling workforce-training programs; and developing "transformative projects" under the banner of Trump's $1 trillion infrastructure plan, such as providing broadband internet service to every American. Kushner has now basically been saddled with several full-time jobs, in which he is responsible for fulfilling many, if not all, of his father-in-law's campaign promises.' (LINKINS. 2017)

There are only so many hours in a day. Even senior executives with years of experience have limits of time, energy and knowledge. So putting a young Real Estate mogul into roles that require incredibly specialized knowledge is a disaster in waiting

For sure, every leader needs to learn the art of delegating, but they also need to understand the difference between delegating and abdicating. In Kushner's case, I think abdication is alive and well with little or no support, training or back up from Trump.

This appointment and Trump's expectations of his young son-in-law are breathtakingly terrifying.

'One of the true tests of leadership is the ability to recognize a problem before it becomes an emergency.'

Arnold H.

Chapter 8

Be careful whose advice you seek

"I will not let oil companies write the country's energy plan or endanger our coastlines or collect another $4b in corporate welfare from our tax payers."

Obama

Lesson 46: Beware conspiracy theorists

Donald Trump and Steve Bannon's Coup in the Making

'Trump campaigned on a platform of unifying the nation, but by striking at the state he and Bannon intend to turn us against each other.' (BEN-GHIAT. 2017)

'Bannon is so dominated by a desire to wage war and vanquish his enemy that he cannot think clearly about the damage wrought by his destructive, polarizing approach or the long-term consequences.' (FRIEDERSDORP. 2016)

Choose your advisors very, very carefully because the people you surround yourself with says everything about you as a leader. Pick a variety of advisors to get a broader view rather than just one person's opinion.

If you surround yourself with 'yes' people then eventually you have a recipe for disaster. Every leader needs people who challenge them. Surrounding yourself with people not quite as smart as you may make you look smarter than the average bear – but it also highlights your personal or professional inadequacies.

The brave leader also surrounds themselves with people who have complementary skills; people who ask great questions without fear or favor and above all they surround themselves with individuals who bring challenging ideas to the mix.

Great leaders have no fear of people who are smarter than themselves, in fact, the wise leader actively recruits them.

Do NOT choose individuals who are conspiracy theorists at heart or who, clearly have their own agendas. They will make you cautious and distrustful of everything and everybody. They will tell you that the only person you can really trust is them, when in fact they are the last people you should trust.

'The simple but true fact of life is that you become like those with whom you closely associate - for the good and the bad.'
Colin Powell

Lesson 47: Be careful whose advice you ignore

TRUMP: I'm a 'smart person,' don't need intelligence briefings every single day

'President-elect Donald Trump brushed off concerns that he's not participating in the traditional daily intelligence and national security briefings that presidents hold every day.

In a rare post-election interview that aired Sunday, Trump argued for why he did not need to receive regular classified intelligence briefings on national security and foreign affairs, saying he told intelligence officials to only brief him when a situation the intelligence community is monitoring changes.

I'm, like, a smart person. I don't have to be told the same thing in the same words every single day for the next eight years," the president-elect added. "I don't need that. But I do say, 'If something should change, let us know.' (TANI. 2016)

If anyone but Trump had said this, I would have agreed. In the early days of a new leadership role, it would be not only a good idea to attend daily briefings, but a good 'look.' Then in time for sure, a leader could start to step back and delegate the responsibility.

If nothing else the leader is getting to know their people and they get to know him or her. Just the act of showing up at such meetings says that the information is relevant, and the people are important. Placing no value on the work completed by your teams has a downstream effect on morale.

Your advisors and their subordinate teams work on compiling those reports so that, a) the leader is in the loop, and b) is less likely to be caught off guard if a situation arises.

Also, consider that in the early days you are getting a feel for what is most important and relevant to the leadership role, what can be delegated to others, what is no longer relevant and finally what is missing.

So, does the leader need to be at such a meeting every day? Absolutely; until your head is firmly in the game, you've delegated what you can and your fingers are on the pulse.

'You know what hurts so much?
It's when someone made you feel special yesterday
but makes you feel like you're a nobody today.'

Not known

Lesson 48: Be very, very, very careful who you get into bed with

Goldman Sachs Is About To Swallow Donald Trump

'In an attempt to rebut reports that he is governing ineffectively and beholden to a small group of fringe right-wing aides, President Donald Trump is reportedly considering yet another White House staff shakeup just 11 weeks into his presidency. Axios and The Wall Street Journal reported on Thursday that Trump is thinking of dismissing or demoting his current chief of staff, Reince Priebus, and his key adviser, Steve Bannon. Both outlets reported that former Goldman Sachs President Gary Cohn — who currently serves as Trump's top economic adviser — is a key contender to replace Priebus.' (CARTER et al. 2017)

NOTE: If you give your opponent (Hillary Clinton) a hard time for being in the pocket of Wall Street; and if one of your promises was to 'drain the swamp' then getting into bed with the very people you ridiculed, isn't a very good look.

◆◆◆◆◆◆◆

Trump's long romance with Russia

'When Donald Trump talks about his desire to have good relations between the U.S. and Russia, it's not a recent attraction. Trump's attempts to expand his business and his brand there date back decades, and this history casts a shadow over his pro-Russian foreign policy. As a presidential candidate, he courts Putin's favor, extending the charm offensive intended to build the Trump real-estate empire.' (ROGIN. 2016)

◆◆◆◆◆◆◆

Trump to Russians in Oval Office: Firing 'nut job' Comey eased pressure, NYT reports

'In an Oval Office meeting last week, President Donald Trump reportedly told Russian diplomats that ex-FBI Director James Comey is a "nut job" and that firing him relieved "great pressure." Trump reportedly said. "I faced great pressure because of Russia. That's taken off."' (PRAMUK. 2017)

◆◆◆◆◆◆◆

White House furious after being trolled with Russia Oval Office Photos

'The White House did not anticipate that the Russian government would allow its state news agency to post photographs of an Oval Office meeting between President Donald Trump, Russian Foreign Minister Sergey Lavrov and Russia's ambassador to the US, a White House official said.

Photos of Wednesday's meeting, taken by a Russian state news media photographer one day after Trump fired FBI Director James Comey amid questions about possible Trump campaign collusion with Moscow, were ultimately posted by Russia's news agency, TASS.' (ACOSTA. 2017)

♦♦♦♦♦♦♦

Trump revealed intelligence secrets to Russians in Oval Office

'President Donald Trump disclosed highly classified information to Russia's foreign minister about a planned Islamic State operation, two U.S. officials said on Monday, plunging the White House into another controversy just months into Trump's short tenure in office.

The intelligence, shared at a meeting last week with Russian Foreign Minister Sergei Lavrov and Russian Ambassador Sergei Kislyak, was supplied by a U.S. ally in the fight against the militant group, both officials with knowledge of the situation said.' (MASON et al. 2017)

As a leader, you need to be clear about the decisions you make which may feel great in the moment; which play to your current audience and even make you feel important, but take the time to think about the effects of those decisions down-track.

What ripples could they cause; who will be affected; what other problems could they create?

Bad decisions can seriously burn you down the track. Be realistic about the long term effects of decisions. It is far easier to deal with a small flame than a raging, out of control, bush fire.

Sadly, when leaders are so deep into their own ego they tend to think they are invincible. Every challenge is a must win. Every person they meet needs to be someone they can beat or impress with their superior knowledge.

There was a very succinct reason why Winston Churchill said, "Loose lips sink ships."

There are some people you simply should not mess with; Putin is probably one of those people.

Interestingly – there is a corollary here for Putin – he thought he could take on the American democratic process by favoring Trump's election at the expense of Hillary Clinton. That is turning out to be a case of him miscalculating and possibly playing one game too many. Because, despite the strange Putin/Trump alleged relationship, new sanctions have been imposed on Russia by the Republican Party; and Congress is implementing creative ways to go around Trump.

♦♦♦♦♦♦♦

Senate Makes It Harder for Trump to Lift Russian Sanctions

'The U.S. Senate voted overwhelmingly on Wednesday for new sanctions punishing Russian Federation for meddling in the 2016 U.S. election, and to force President Donald Trump to get Congress' approval before easing any existing sanctions.' (GROSS.2017)

♦♦♦♦♦♦♦

Russia Calls Off Talks with United States Because of New Sanctions

'Russia cancelled talks with a top US official to protest the latest sanctions punishing Russian companies and individuals over the conflict in Ukraine, in a fresh setback for President Donald Trump's bid to improve ties with President Vladimir Putin's government.' (BLOOMBERG. 2017)

I once heard someone say that before we make a shady decision, we should think about what the headline would look like in a newspaper or on social media. Or worse, what would it feel like to be in jail for several years.

If you as a business owner have been doing a few shady deals and someone finds out (which they will) then attacking the source won't make it go away and won't make your part in what has happened look any better. In fact lashing out at the source makes you look even worse.

Be extremely careful who you get into 'bed' with. Don't let your ego blind you to the fact that some 'deals' are simply too dangerous. Walking away is OK.

'Americans Will Always Do the Right Thing –
After Exhausting All the Alternatives'
Churchill

Chapter 9

Build an exciting future rather than attempting to resurrect an obsolete past

'It's not so much that we are afraid of change
or so in love with the old ways,
it's the place in between we fear
...it's like the space between trapezes.'

Maralyn Ferguson

Lesson 49: Don't let every step you take, be a step backward

Donald Trump's Tax Plan Would Make the Rich Richer, Uncle Sam Poorer

'The way Donald Trump would like, would be to spend a hundred million dollars building a new bridge in the highway. Then he would like to sell it, privatize it to a private buyer like himself, for 10 million dollars. So the government would spend a huge amount of money that could've been used for a free bridge or a free road. He'll then sell it for 10 million dollars to a private owner, who will put up a toll booth and charge money for coming across, and make a mint.' (HUDSON. 2017)

◆◆◆◆◆◆◆

A budget is a moral document: the one Trump produced is dark

'A presidential budget isn't so much a policy proposal as a statement of an administration's moral vision for the country. The budget presented by President Donald Trump on Thursday is a document fundamentally unconcerned with the government's role in improving the plight of its most vulnerable citizens. That message is clear in the budget's topline proposals and its deeper details. Trump calls for a $54 billion boost in defense spending and immigration enforcement. More border patrol agents, more Immigration and Customs Enforcement officers, more fighter jets that don't work, and a border wall with Mexico. To offset those fresh expenses, he wants to take an ax to a host of anti-poverty programs — everything from public housing to food programs helping elderly people with disabilities.

This was an ideological choice. When explaining why it would eliminate a $35 million affordable housing program, the administration declared the endeavor simply wasn't the government's business: "This program is duplicative of efforts funded by philanthropy and other more flexible private sector investments. Republicans have long believed that communities, religious groups and volunteer organizations are often best equipped to help those in need. But many of them still acknowledge government has some role to play in these endeavors. Over the years, for example, they have supported AmeriCorps — a national service program that Trump's budget would eliminate.' (CARTER. 2017)

And from the Washington Post;

'It's very easy to look at a laundry list of things that exist and say, 'Cut, cut, cut, cut,' and say, 'Well, this is wasteful spending' without really understanding the true impact," said Durant City Manager Tim Rundel, who grew up in poverty in northwest Arkansas. "The bottom line is a lot of our citizens depend on those programs."

Betty Harris, 77, gets choked up when she talks about her husband, who died in May, and her son, who died in February. Her two daughters live in Oklahoma City and visit once a month or so. There are two things that get her to leave her home: a quilting circle with friends and daily visits to the senior center. The center offers lunch for two bucks, exercise classes, gospel singalongs, tax preparation help, monthly boxes of food for low-income seniors, a meal delivery program and a staff that can patiently explain Medicare or how to operate a cellphone. If some-one doesn't show up, the others quickly figure out why. "It's the only bright spot," said Harris, who used to work for AT&T. "It makes me get dressed and get out of the house."' (JOHNSON. 2017)

◆◆◆◆◆◆◆

Trump and the One Percent. Making The Super Rich Even Richer

'So part of the reason the stock market has gone up is that corporate raiders have borrowed very inexpensively, at say 1% or a bit more from a bank, and bought companies whose dividend rates are 3% or 4 or 5%. They're after what's called the arbitrage, the difference in the two rates. So you take over a company with borrowed money. As a result of paying interest to the banks and this bor-rowed money, you don't have to pay income tax on it because this is counted as a cost of doing business, not as a cost of takeover.

The first thing they do is tighten working conditions. They work labor harder. They let the labor force go. When people retire, they don't hire new workers. They just work the remaining workers all the more. So, what's happened isn't a new investment. It's just the opposite. It's disinvestment. It's asset stripping. What creates the stock market going up is not capital formation. It's asset strip-ping. When Donald Trump calls that wealth creation, it means his wealth – mean-ing the money he's been able to make. But that money has been made by mak-ing the economy poorer.' (HUDSON. 2017)

◆◆◆◆◆◆◆

With Trump steering America backwards, China is ready to take the lead on climate

'In the coming years, the opposite dynamic is poised to play out. U.S. President Donald Trump's signing of an executive order on Tuesday aimed at undoing many of the Obama administration's climate change policies flips the roles of the two powers. Now, it is far likelier that the world will see China pushing the United States to meet its commitments and try to live up to the letter and spirit of the 2015 Paris Agreement, even if Trump has signalled he has no intention of doing so.' (WONG. 2017)

———————————————————

Rod Oram, a New Zealand journalist who writes on corporate, economic and political issues; and is a regular broadcaster on NZ radio and television made the following observations at one of my forums, on what he believes the Trump administration will do to America:

- World view: America First

- Trade: We win, you lose

- Taxes: Rich win, poor lose

- Economy: Back to the 1950s

- Foreign policy: Back to1940s

- Culture: Back to 1850s

- Politics: Divide & conquer

- Congress: Manipulate

- Judiciary: Discredit

- Temperament: VolatileThe number one task of a leader is surely, to take their business or country forward. Yes futures are uncertain. In an ever changing nano-second world leaders need their fingers on the pulse of every challenge likely to hit them. It is their function to be working on every opportunity likely to come their way so they can educate and encourage their followers to plan and prepare.

Going backwards is absolutely not an option. It may sound great to your followers when you tell them that you will keep them safe and protected, but safety is an illusion and you can't protect people from progress, in fact you are doing them a dis-service even attempting to do that.

A leader lights the way into the future; takes them on the journey; communicates every step of the way. Reminds them of the reasons they are going forward, and that going backward is not an option.

The dream begins with a teacher who believes in you,
who tugs and pushes and leads you to the next plateau,
sometimes poking you with a sharp stick called 'truth'.

Dan Rather

Chapter 10

Think through the legacy you will leave and how you will be remembered

"If you would not be forgotten
as soon as you are dead,
either write something worth reading
or do something worth writing."

Benjamin Franklin

Lesson 50: You create the history you will be judged by

The greatest of all lessons in leadership is to remember that you are not simply making day to day decisions; you are creating history; a history that you will eventually be judged by. Period! Remember always that there is more than just the here and now; more than the power you briefly wield; more than just the deals you cut and the money you accumulate. History will draw up its ledger and the leader assigned their place or simply forgotten.

Because we are dealing with the subject of leadership using President Trump as our example it is only fair that we use American Presidents as our list of best and worst leaders. So that each is measured from the same scorecard of leadership characteristics as the basis of the ranking.

The Ten Best and Worst American Presidents

The following list is compiled from the [1]2017 C-SPAN Survey, conducted by the National Cable Satellite Corporation. Scored by a panel of ninety-one historians and other professional observers each President was scored against their effectiveness or skill in the following areas;

- Public Persuasion

- Crisis Leadership

- Economic Management

- Moral Authority

- International Relations

- Administrative Skills

- Relations with Congress

- Vision / Setting an Agenda

- Pursued Equal Justice For All

- Performance Within Context of Times

	BEST	WORST
10	Johnson, L. B.	Van Buren
9	Reagan	Arthur
8	Kennedy	Hoover
7	Jefferson	Fillmore
6	Truman	Harrison, W. H.
5	Eisenhower	Tyler
4	Roosevelt, T.	Harding
3	Roosevelt, F. D.	Pierce
2	Washington	Johnson, A.
1	**Lincoln**	**Buchanan**

At the time of the survey, Trump had yet to be added to the president's lists. As an aside note, George W Bush (jr.) was ranked eleventh worst President, while Obama came in at twelfth best.

The key characteristic of those leaders that made the 'best' list is that they rose above personal agendas and self-interest.

Always remember that the decisions you make and the actions you take (or don't take) will live in people's memories for a very long time. If your name becomes associated with all that is wrong with being in leadership, then your children and your grandchildren will be lumbered with your legacy.

In country leadership, some things have to be above party politics: healthcare, education, care for the less fortunate and worker safety must be bi-partisan. No-one should benefit financially from these services. No vested interests should be allowed to tamper with what are essentially the basics of a functioning society.

"Pick a leader who will make their citizens proud. One who will stir the hearts of the people, so that the sons and daughters of a given nation strive to emulate their leader's greatness. Only then will a nation be truly great, when a leader inspires and produces citizens worthy of becoming future leaders, honorable decision makers and peacemakers. And in these times, a great leader must be extremely brave. Their leadership must be steered only by their conscience, not a bribe."

Suzy Kassem, Rise Up and Salute the Sun: The Writings of Suzy Kassem

---

i. Presidential Historians Survey 2017. https://www.c-span.org/presidentsurvey2017/

Chapter 11

Dealing with the Elephants in the Room

"There's a phrase, "the elephant in the living room," which purports to describe what it's like to live with a drug addict, an alcoholic, an abuser. People outside such relationships will sometimes ask, "How could you let such a business go on for so many years? Didn't you see the elephant in the living room?" And it's so hard for anyone living in a more normal situation to understand the answer that comes closest to the truth; "I'm sorry, but it was there when I moved in. I didn't know it was an elephant; I thought it was part of the furniture." There comes an aha-moment for some folks - the lucky ones - when they suddenly recognize the difference."

Stephen King

Elephant One: Using the Cover of Darkness to send out Controversial Decisions

Trump gives new meaning to the Friday night news dump, enraging his critics

'As a monster hurricane not seen on American shores in over a decade bore down on Texas on Friday night, a tsunami of news out of Washington was also on its way.' (PHILLIP. 2017)

I was putting the finishing touches to the 50 lessons feeling pretty sure that there wasn't much else that Donald could do to shock me. And once again, he proved me wrong. He very cynically used the early stages of a massive hurricane about to hit the Texas coast to slide through three polarizing decisions:

1. He fired the controversial national security adviser Sebastian Gorka (though Gorka insists he resigned).

2. He signed the bill banning transgenders from the military.

3. He pardoned the controversial Arizona Sheriff – Joe Arpaio.

◆◆◆◆◆◆◆

Statement on Trump's Neo-Nazi Adviser Seb Gorka

'As Trump remembers the six million Jews and millions of others killed by Nazis during the Holocaust, it serves as a reminder that Seb Gorka, whose affiliation to a Neo-Nazi group is well-documented and goes back decades, still serves as an adviser to Trump.

"Unless Trump fires Gorka, nothing he says today should be taken seriously. Gorka should not have any place in the White House, let alone be advising Trump on matters of national security. It's long past time for him to go."' (Editorial. 2017)

◆◆◆◆◆◆◆

Trump to reinstate US military ban on transgender people

'The study put the number of transgender people in the military between 1,320 and 6,630. Gender-change surgery is rare in the general population, and the RAND study estimated the possibility of 30 to 140 new hormone treatments a year in the military, with 25 to 130 gender transition-related surgeries among active service members. The cost could range from $2.4 million and $8.4 million, an amount that would represent an "exceedingly small proportion" of total health care expenditures, the study found'. (DIAMOND. 2017)

♦♦♦♦♦♦♦

President Trump pardons former Sheriff Joe Arpaio

President Trump has pardoned former Sheriff Joe Arpaio from his criminal contempt conviction, removing the only legal consequences the lawman faced stemming from a racial-profiling suit. (CASSIDY. 2017)

———————————————

It isn't unknown for politicians to push controversial decisions through just before a long weekend or government shut down when everyone is distracted. Sadly it seems to be a norm. All three decisions Donald made seem to plunge to depths of even greater significance when you consider what motivated them.

If we look at the transgender ban first, the costs involved with having these incredibly brave people fighting for America seems minuscule. As one general commented, "these costs are just 'rounding' amounts in context of the massive military budget."

Transgender people are doubly brave when you consider that not only are they putting their lives on the line for their country, but they must deal with all manner of backlash on a daily basis because of their sexual orientation. So why is Donald fixated on something that the military has no problem with? And what cost to the services when these people are sent home? Who will replace their skills and knowledge? What will be the cost of training people to take their places and how long will that take? And how will the current personnel deployed in dangerous situations manage without them?

Another Donald decision that makes absolutely no sense at all. Was he just on another of his power trips? Or was it that on top of all the other prejudices he displays, Donald now shows us that he is also homophobic?

When we couple the Gorka firing/resignation with the Arpaio pardoning, we surely see a conflict for his beloved base. I'm sure they will be delighted that he has pardoned Arpaio who was in contempt of court and facing jail for his abusive treatment of Latino's; though they will surely be confused that he has fired Gorka who appears to be everything they want in an adviser to their chosen leader.

Trump may have slipped these decisions out while people were otherwise engaged with the hurricane, but there will be a day of reckoning.

"Nearly all men can stand adversity
but if you want to test a man's character,
give him power."
Abe Lincoln

Elephant Two: Failing to test a person's fitness for office

From that very first day I laughed when I heard Donald was going on the campaign trail to today (day 209 of his presidency) I've been pondering the following questions:

- Why is submitting tax returns not mandatory for anyone who goes on the presidential trail? Yes, it's laudable to trust the candidates, and probably most of them are trust-worthy but just in case – then playing 'nice' doesn't cut it when the successful person has so much financial power. Submitting tax returns should be 100% not negotiable. No tax returns = no campaign trail. That would have stopped Donald at the starting gate I would suspect. His businesses have been made bankrupt four times; he had a reputation for not paying suppliers; he was knee deep in numerous lawsuits so why would anyone think this was a good person to be managing the country's finances?[1]

- Why are candidates not put through rigorous medical tests? This is another aspect of taking office that really is just common sense. In Donald's case, he is 71 years old and over-weight; it sounds as though he doesn't have a great diet and he abhors exercise. A thorough medical would have probably been another of those deciding factors for declining his application to stand for office.

- Why are candidates not psychologically assessed? Any baseline profiling tool would have set off warning signals that Donald was a person with alarming behavioral conflicts; bullying tendencies; a distinct scarcity of empathy and even the possibility of personality disorders.

'He Puts The World At Risk': Psychiatrists Unite Against Trump in Letter to Congress

'A group of psychiatrists have taken to Congress with a letter commenting on President Donald Trump's mental health. They think he poses a "clear and present danger to the world".' (TOUREILLE. 2017)

- Why was there nothing in place before or during the election campaign to stop a 'Donald' type of personality becoming president? Everything anyone needed to know about Donald was there for the world to see long before he went on the campaign trail. He had a shocking reputation with women; he held grievances; he proudly paid people back 10 fold, and he minimized, marginalized and abused anyone of color at every opportunity. After all, a person can't get much lower than to mock someone who is handicapped.

- Why does America still have the Electoral College system? If voting had been left to the American people, which is surely what a democracy is all about, then Hillary Clinton would have been the President. She beat Donald by 3 million votes. And popular or not, she would never have created the chaos he causes on a daily basis. Shame on the Electoral College.

A shift in even one of the practices above could have saved America from Donald Trump. Sadly they didn't, which brings me to two more elephants in the room:

- Why are the majority of Republicans staying stubbornly silent during the constant unsavory situations he seems hell-bent on creating?

- What does he actually have to do to cross the line that would invoke the 25th Amendment?

"The first responsibility of a leader is to define reality.
The last is to say thank you. In between, the leader is a servant."

- Max DePree -

In the final analysis

No-one ever said that being a leader was easy. It's a tough job, and it surely isn't for the faint-hearted. Whether you are leading a team of five or find yourself at the head of a country, you will be tested and challenged at every turn. In the end, leadership surely is about helping your followers deal with the stresses of an ever-changing and sometimes scary world.

All countries around the globe are facing similar challenges, and we really do need to elect transformational leaders. People who can see the road ahead and can take people with them.

In America, you would have thought that the Democratic Party would have been right onto this loss of jobs challenge. Many of the people who switched to voting for Trump were historically Democratic voters. You could say 'serves the Democrats right' because it seems they absolutely took their eye of their own voters. They got complacent, and complacency in leadership is the ultimate death knell.

So as a result of complacency and the strange voting system in America, we now have Donald as POTUS. I still can't make up my mind whether Trump wants to be a dictator or a martyr. He certainly identifies with, glorifies or displays similar pathological traits to some strange people both current and historic:

• Putin

• Bashar Al Assad

• Kim Jong Un

• Recep Tayyip Erdogan

Dictators all.

So if he can't be a dictator, and he can't, then it is safe to say that Donald will ultimately play the martyr card. As he fails to put into place any of his promises, he will eventually start telling his voters that it isn't his fault that the wall won't be built; or health reform can't be implemented. It's all the fault of those nasty Republicans in Senate (the party he is supposed to be the leader of) who keep blocking his great ideas. And if only they would give him free reign, he would seriously make America great again!

It's also becoming increasingly clear that we have two 'Trumps' – the 'teleprompter Trump' who has his speeches written for him in careful and considered language. When he sticks to the script, he actually sounds presidential. And there's 'loose cannon' Trump who goes off on rants about everything from the fake press to his inauguration crowd. This is the real Trump.

But it feels 100% inevitable that his own personality will eventually bring about his demise.

As his ratings fall and his promises don't materialize; when the people who voted for him realize that he is the worst version of a salesman – lots of promises and very few deliveries, then people will start walking away from him.

Surely?

In the meantime, we are left with more questions than answers as to how this Trump roller coaster will end.

- [i]Will Charlottesville be Trump's Watergate?

- [ii]Will those tax returns finally show up and lead to impeachment?

- [iii]Will the Mueller investigation find those Russian connections and force his resignation?

- [iv]Will Kim Jong Un be his undoing?

- [v]Will the Republican party turn against him and invoke the 25th amendment?

---

i. Marina Fang. Huffpost. 14/8/2017 - http://www.huffingtonpost.com/entry/trump-white-house-response-charlottesville_us_59908c5ce4b090964297cdf5?ncid=engmodushpmg00000003
ii. Alexander Burns and Johathan Martin. The New York Times. 22/8/2017 - https://www.nytimes.com/2017/08/22/us/politics/mitch-mcconnell-trump.html?smid=fb-share
iii. Maggie Haberman, Michael D. Shear and Glen Thrush. The New York Times. 18/8/2017 - https://www.nytimes.com/2017/08/18/us/politics/steve-bannon-trump-white-house.html?action=click&contentCollection=Politics&module=RelatedCoverage&region=Marginalia&pgtype=article
iv. Evan Perez, Pamela Brown and Shimon Prokupecz. CNN. 4/8/2017 - http://edition.cnn.com/2017/08/03/politics/mueller-investigation-russia-trump-one-year-financial-ties/index.html
v. Rebecca Shapiro. Huffpost. 23/8/2017 - http://www.huffingtonpost.com/entry/james-clapper-trump-dark-warning-nuclear-codes_us_599d1d09e4b0d97c3ffff602?ncid=engmodushpmg00000003

Chapter 12

There will be Life after Trump

'We don't even know how strong we are until we are forced to bring that hidden strength forward. In times of tragedy, of war, of necessity,
people do amazing things. The human capacity for survival and renewal is awesome.'

Isabel Allende

No matter how long it takes, at some stage, Trump's presidency will, I'm sure, be just a fascinating blip in history. What his rise to fame taught us, hopefully – is that anyone who is going into a position of leadership should be vetted to within an inch of their lives; financially, physically and psychologically.

In the interim, however, we need to make sense of what we have all witnessed since his inauguration and to put context around this traumatic administration, so the same mistakes are not made again. We need to do this, not just for the sake of America and her reputation but for the safety and security of rest of the world. Because putting a person who seems to be having a permanent two-year-old tantrum anywhere near those nuclear codes surely puts the whole world at risk.

And we must never lose sight of the bigger picture that Donald seems to have washed his hands of.

At the global level leaders need to consider the next stage of our development as a human race; to acknowledge that climate change is real; to find ways to deal with an ever-growing population; to re-invigorate failing communities; to re-train the people who are going to be put on the scrap heap; to foresee and plan for the effects of whole industries being replaced by technology. To find a solution to North Korea and to work out what causes people to become terrorists.

The Good News

Democracy IS working albeit slowly. It appears that most people thought he would eventually grow into the role given time. He isn't; he won't and he can't. So although it appears to have taken way too long for leaders around America to stand up to Trump, it is quietly starting to happen:

Chicago To Sue Trump Administration Over Sanctuary City Funding Threat

'Chicago will sue the Trump administration on Monday over threats to withhold public safety grant money from so-called sanctuary cities, escalating a pushback against a federal immigration crackdown, Mayor Rahm Emanuel announced on Sunday.' (KENNING, AX. 2017)

Donald Trump Signs Russia Sanctions Bill He Calls 'Significantly Flawed'

'President Donald Trump has signed a bill that allows new sanctions against Russia, but not without expressing his concerns over what he considers "significantly flawed" legislation.' (LAVENDAR. 2017)

These Republicans are speaking out against Trump's Transgender Ban.[1]

* Sen. Joni Ernst (Iowa)

* Sen. Orrin Hatch (Utah)

* Sen. John McCain (Arizona)

* Sen. Richard Shelby (Alabama)

* Rep. Ileana Ros-Lehtinen (Florida)

* Caitlyn Jenner

President Donald Trump should not have pardoned a former Arizona sheriff who was convicted of criminal contempt in a case of racial profiling, the Republican speaker of the House of Representatives, Paul Ryan, said on Saturday.[2]

♦♦♦♦♦♦♦

Standing Up to Trump is Good for Business

Companies want stability and virtue-by-association.
This president provides neither.
(STRAIN. BLOOMBERG. 2017)

The really good news

What was smart about Donald is that he tapped into the pain of the middle classes. He was a man who knew his base and told them exactly what they wanted and needed to hear.

The 'Make America Great Again' slogan was sheer brilliance. The change his base wanted to see was a return to their own glory days when they had jobs and pride and self-respect. The days when they truly were the backbone of the American workforce. I'll deal with his 'alt-right' supporters later; their needs were very different.

The rust belt had been neglected and ignored, and they were now deservedly angry. He tapped into that hurt and pain and used it to further his own agenda, but now at least, America knows what these voters want, then whoever steps into the POTUS role next, knows exactly what they have to do to deliver.

The not so great news

I felt from day one of the campaigns that Donald's agenda was never to make America Great Again; it was to make America white again. Hence the rise and rise of the 'supremacy' groups – the 'alt-right'?

What do they actually want? Is it simply to be right and to be white? If it is then that is really sad. Being white is no guarantee of anything. I've met some really smart white people, and I've met some incredibly dumb white people. And ditto for any race.

Or is their need something even deeper and sadder than that? Are they like soccer hooligans who are actually not even remotely interested in soccer – they just want to create havoc; be noticed; be powerful; be scary? And why do they do that? Because deep down they have no meaningful purpose in their lives. They are empty. Violence makes them feel alive.

Who Are Trump's Alt-Right Supporters?
(ROSEN. 2016)

When we viewed those neo-Nazi marches in Charlottesville, anyone who has had parents or grandparents who were slaves; or who fought the Nazi's; or have families who died in concentration camps; or people with any modicum of decency and humanity would have just three words.

Shut. Them. Down.

Society needs to make them illegal; to cut them off from their guns and white supremacy supplies; to cut off their freedom; to shut down their websites and at every opportunity to educate, educate, educate. The young man who drove the car into a crowd in Charlottesville killing young Heather Heyer and injuring many more had shown tendencies even at a school age of being troubled. So identify these people early and find ways to educate and un-radicalize them.

Sadly the people who relate to such groups are not unlike Donald J Trump. They are bullies, they marginalize; they are 'ists' of the worst kind – racists; misogynists, etc.

I'd suggest conscripting them into the army if they want a fight. And if they are serious about fighting for their country, a term in Afghanistan might make them realize the privileged lives they already have. But the armed services wouldn't want their kind because basically, such people are the worst kind of cowards. Like most cowards, they can only be brave when they are surrounded by their ilk. Didn't Donald dodge the draft five times and yet had the audacity to call Senator John McCain a loser because he was captured and endured several years in a prisoner of war camp?

Donald Trump's Draft Deferments:
Four for College, One for Bad Feet
(EDER. 1/8/2017)

The exceptionally good news

Goodwill always overcome evil though sometimes it just takes time to wake people up to what is really happening around them. Democracy will finally overcome apathy. The truth will always be the truth, and good men (and women) will eventually step up; stand up and speak up.

Boston Fights Back Against White Supremacy

'Just a week after Charlottesville, over 40,000 counter-protesters took to the streets in Boston, greatly outnumbering the 50 attendees at the "Free Speech Rally" organized by a group with white supremacists affiliation.' (JAYNE. 2017)

---

[3]Heather Heyer died standing up for what she firmly believed in. She was literally run down by a white supremacist in Charlottesville. Her brave mother [4]Susan Bro makes it our duty to speak up when she said "They tried to kill my child to shut her up, well, guess what? You just magnified her."

So let's magnify Heather Heyer every day going forward by standing up to the bullies; the white supremacists and the neo-Nazis. Let's not stay silent when we hear things that go against our fundamental values. Let's light candles instead of torches and let's never sit by while flag bearing neo-Nazi's march in our towns and our cities.

The world needs transformational leaders. People who can see the road ahead and can take people with them. America under Trump seems to have washed its hands of these bigger issues which is a tragedy. But the world will go on, with or without Donald.

I just have to leave the last word to Simone Veil – a Holocaust survivor:

"It's here, where absolute evil was perpetrated, that the will must resurface for a fraternal world, a world based on respect of man and his dignity."

TO BE CONTINUED...

---

1. Tim Molloy, The Wrap. 26/7/2017 - http://www.thewrap.com/heres-a-list-of-republicans-smart-enough-to-split-with-trump-on-his-transgender-military-ban/
2. Patrick Rucker, HuffPost. 26/8/2017 - http://www.huffingtonpost.com/entry/paul-ryan-trump-arpaio-pardon_us_59a23598e4b05710aa5cb18a?ncid=inblnkushpmg00000009
3. Steve Almasy and Chandrika Narayan, CNN. 16/8/2017 - http://edition.cnn.com/2017/08/13/us/charlottesville-heather-heyer-profile/index.html
4. Alison Durkee, Mic. 17/8/2017 - https://mic.com/articles/183859/heather-heyers-mom-gives-stirring-funeral-speech-this-is-just-the-beginning-of-heathers-legacy#.Nzm6tiCKr

Recommended Reading

- Hundreds Claim Donald Trump Doesn't Pay His Bills in Full - https://www.nbcnews.com/news/us-news/hundreds-claim-donald-trump-doesn-t-pay-his-bills-n589261

- A Trip Down Donald Trump's Bankruptcy Memory Lane - https://www.forbes.com/sites/debtwire/2015/08/18/a-trip-down-donald-trumps-bankruptcy-memory-lane/#674893ef4609

- Donald Trump Mocks Reporter With Disability - http://edition.cnn.com/videos/tv/2015/11/26/donald-trump-mocks-reporter-with-disability-berman-sot-ac.cnn

- Twenty-fifth Amendment to the United States Constitution - https://en.wikipedia.org/wiki/Twenty-fifth_Amendment_to_the_United_States_Constitution

The 5 Levels of Leadership - **by John C Maxwell**

7 Habits of Highly Effective People - **by Steven R.Covey**

Start with Why - **by Simon Sinek**

The Leadership Gap: what gets between you and your greatness - **by Lolly Daskal**

The Servant: a simple story about the essence of true leadership - **by James C Hunter**

Other Titles by Ann Andrews

My Dear Franchisees...

If you are a franchisor, a franchisee or a manager, then this book is a must read...

Ann Andrews asks the question – as a franchisor would it make your life easier if your franchisees realized that:
- They have not bought a job?
- You are not their Mum, their Dad or their banker?
- You are absolutely not their enemy?

Carl Davies asks would it also make your life easier to know before your franchisees sign up:
- Exactly what their strengths and weaknesses are?
- Exactly what motivates them?
- Exactly what help they will need to make their business a success?
- Whether they will be suitable franchisees at all?

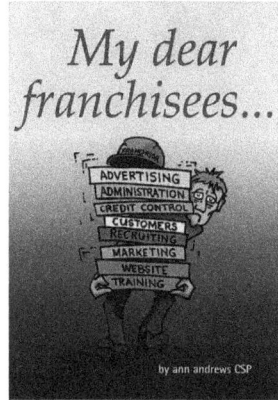

Finding the Square Root of a Banana

In today's business world, where resources are strained, stress has become a way of life and every organization is trying to do more with less on a daily basis, it is clear we cannot work in the hierarchical, parent/child ways of the past. Many organizations have tried to hand over day-to-day decision making to employees, experimented with self-managed teams. And unfortunately, the results have been under-whelming at best, and a nightmare at worst. In this book you will learn to turn whinging, whining groups into highly-focused teams in a few simple steps!

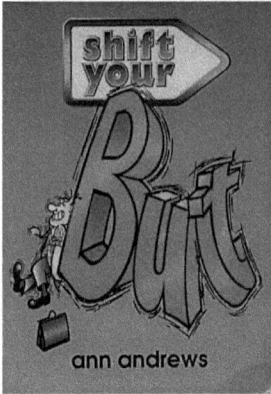

Shift Your But!

This book introduces fresh concepts and thinking to the area of business management. The author's basic premise is that our current work methods are left over from the industrial revolution - and so are our results.

In the chaotic, ever-changing world we live in and where in the next 5-10 years the global marketplace will become a totally flat playing field, where no organization will have any product or service that their competitors do not have, Ann Andrews challenges organizations to:

- Free up management time by at least 30% so that managers can work ON the business instead of IN the business
- Move from Parent/Child attitudes into Adult/Adult transactions
- Rethink the way they view work
- And create an ownership rather than a dependency mentality.
- The author shares with the reader the first steps towards thriving in business instead of merely surviving.

Did I Really Employ You?

A practical, easy-to-use manual to help employers and human resource personnel select the right person for the job.

- Topics include designing the ideal candidate, defining the position and the results you're looking for, using application forms to save time, and conducting effective job interviews.
- Did I Really Employ You? is a comprehensive guide to getting it right every time.

For more information visit - www.annandrews.co.nz

Bonus Chapter of Ann's next book
'Before It's Too late'

LESSONS IN FOLLOWERSHIP

Definition: 'Followership is a straightforward concept. It is the ability to take direction well, to get in line behind a program, to be part of a team and to deliver on what is expected of you. It gets a bit of a bad rap! How well the followers follow is probably just as important to enterprise success as how well the leaders lead.' John S.McCallum

We expect an awful lot from our leaders but do we ever consider what type of 'followers' we are?

I've noticed particularly when a country leader is elected, how quickly their allure appears to wear off and how rapidly their voters turn against them. President Macron of France is a perfect example. He rode into power on a wave of patriotic enthusiasm and within a very short space of time found his popularity waning.

Headline: Darling of Europe, disaster at home: Emmanuel Macron struggles in polls as voters turn

Extract: More than half of French people questioned disapprove of the French's President's performance, according to the Ipsos Game Changers poll for French daily Le Point. Of those surveyed, 54 per cent were "dissatisfied" with the 39-year-old's actions, less than six months after his landslide victory against far-right leader Marine Le Pen. 58 per cent of voters questioned in the Ipsos poll said France was "neither better nor worse off" since Mr Macron was sworn in as president in May.

Why is that? Why do we turn against our leaders so rapidly? Are we followers too impatient or do we just have unrealistic expectations of what is possible and how long things will take?

Don't we as followers, have a responsibility to trust the people we have elected? Shouldn't we at least give them breathing space to settle into the role? Or is it that once we've voted for something we then wish we hadn't and so we attack the person or system rather than look in the mirror and question why we voted for that person or process in the first place?

Brexit is a living breathing example of overnight voter remorse. Apparently the very day after the leave/stay referendum, more than 1 million people regretted their vote and wanted to have an opportunity to change their vote. There are no second chances in referendums so we must make sure we can live with and by our vote. We must take time to check the facts.

So do we as followers have to do a bit of 'growing up'?

Back to the election of Donald Trump. To be fair, it seems that for a small group of his followers, he can do nothing wrong, however, his base is also shrinking as many of the things he promised he would do, remain undone.

Headline: Trump hits new polling low as base shrinks

Extract: Only 40 percent of registered voters approve of the job Trump is doing as president, the new POLITICO/Morning Consult poll shows, down from a high-water mark of 52 percent in March. And the percentage who approve strongly — one way to measure the size of Trump's most fervent supporters — is also at a new low: just 18 percent.

As followers I believe these are our responsibilities in elections:

- To thoroughly research the leader we are voting for; their past behaviours; reputation and credibility; to look beyond the glitz and glamour.

- In the case of American voters, to not just follow one source of information i.e. Fox News v CNN but to explore all of the reputable sources before we make a decision, and then having made our decision based on good research to stick with it and give the person a chance. We must absolutely beware of all sources of fake news and avoid listening to conspiracy theorists: they will seriously mess with our heads.

- As voters, we are adults, not children. We need to stop looking for someone to be our Mother or Father our guardian or our keeper.

- To be willing to hear the harsh truth. Trump promised to bring jobs back – a great thought. As an example he promised to re-open coal mines. This for coal miners who had been put onto the scrap heap as mines closed, must have been joy to their ears. But coal is becoming increasingly obsolete as newer and cleaner technologies take over. Did the coal miners really believe this promise? Did they take the initiative after the closures of the mines to look for work in other sectors and perhaps even in other cities. Did they take any responsibility for their own upskilling and re-training – yes there would have been a cost involved to do this, but the cost of not upskilling and being put out of work with obsolete skills doesn't hold much of a future. Sadly as human we don't like to hear the truth – and yet surely, that is the very thing our leaders should be arming us with?

- The greatest responsibility of all? To show up and actually use our vote

Headline: Registered Voters Who Stayed Home Probably Cost Clinton The Election

Extract: Registered voters who didn't vote on Election Day in November were more Democratic-leaning than the registered voters who turned out, according to a post-election poll from Survey Monkey, shared with FiveThirtyEight. In fact, Donald Trump probably would have lost to Hillary Clinton had Republican- and Democratic-leaning registered voters cast ballots at equal rates.

That really concerns me; particularly as a percentage of those no-show voters would have been young women. As women I think we have an even greater responsibility to vote; women died for us to have the right, in some countries women still don't have a vote.

I've been pretty harsh on Trump in my previous book 'Lessons in Leadership: 50 ways to avoid the 'Trump' trap, and I make absolutely no apologies for that. I think he is an appalling leader and I'll continue to voice that opinion until such times as he either improves (which is highly unlikely given his personality) or is replaced, removed or resigns (another thing that is highly unlikely).

If we've taken on a job where our manager turns out to be a monster we can leave and find another job. It isn't so easy when we are faced with a country leader who seems to delight in finding a daily war to fight, either within his own party or with allies or even with other countries.

Alexis de Tocqueville, a French political thinker and historian who wrote the book Democracy in America suggested that sometimes we get the leaders we deserve. So when choosing a leader in an election, we absolutely have a responsibility. We may think one vote won't make a difference, but a vote here and a vote there mounts up and really does make a difference.

I believe that casting a vote is actually a sacred responsibility. Our vote is the most precious gift we have. Use it wisely. Be a great follower.

Be careful what you ask for, you may just get it. Anon

References:
i.   http://www.independent.co.uk/news/uk/politics/brexit-news-second-eu-referendum-leave-voters-regret-bregret-choice-in-millions-a7113336.html
ii.   https://www.ipsos.com/sites/default/files/ct/news/documents/2017-10/globaladvisor_Religion_Charts_US%20FINAL_0.pdf
iii: https://iveybusinessjournal.com/publication/followership-the-other-side-of-leadership/
iv: http://www.express.co.uk/news/world/868603/emmanuel-macron-eu-brussels-summit-2017-october-polls
v: http://www.politico.com/story/2017/08/09/trump-polls-base-polling-241425
vi: https://fivethirtyeight.com/features/registered-voters-who-stayed-home-probably-cost-clinton-the-election/
vii: https://en.wikiquote.org/wiki/Alexis_de_Tocqueville
viii: https://en.wikipedia.org/wiki/Democracy_in_America
viii: https://www.surveymonkey.com/
https://en.wikipedia.org/wiki/Voting_gender_gap_in_the_United_States
http://time.com/4566748/hillary-clinton-firewall-women/

Bibliography

Prologue
              Jennifer Post. Business News Daily. 29/3/2017 - https://goo.gl/2D7Prc

Chapter One
Lesson 1   Patrick Healey and Jonathan Martin. NY Times. 9/10/2016 - https://goo.gl/m7QPNK
Lesson 2   Michael Gerson. Washington Post. 27/9/2016 - https://goo.gl/Jrejtq
              Jennifer Clibbon. CBC News. 06/02/2016 https://goo.gl/JtcsgX
              Gwenda Blair (quotes). Euronews - https://goo.gl/8Qr5Qp Investopedia - https://goo.gl/yxi2hr
Lesson 3   Emily Stephenson and Scott Malone. AOL News. 21/1/2017 - https://goo.gl/a7rNFT
              Jenna Johnson. Washington Post. 29/6/2017 - https://goo.gl/ekBYgB
Lesson 4   Jeremy Diamond. CNN. 1/6/2016 - https://goo.gl/p98PpA
              Aaron Rupar. Think Progress. 10/5/2017 - https://goo.gl/CtgoEP
              Tara Palmeri. Politico. 25/5/2017 - https://goo.gl/u2bHvS
              Hayley Miller. Huffpost. 28/6/2017 - https://goo.gl/QeCjFx
              Josh Dawson, Eliana Johnson and Alex Isenstadt. Politico. 2017 - https://goo.gl/idoRdT

Chapter Two
Lesson 5   Kim Hjelmgaard. USA Today. 20/10/2017 - https://goo.gl/cks9yv
              Geoff Earle. Deputy US Political Editor. Daily Mail 18/3/2017 - https://goo.gl/mtM9uH
              Editorial. WDRB New. 13/5/2017 - https://goo.gl/B84bep
Lesson 6   Phil Houston and Don Tennant. Law Newz 4/3/2016 - https://goo.gl/bGuGcL
              Susan Seager. The Wrap. 23/6/2017 - https://goo.gl/Wz1pbG
Lesson 7   Phil McCausland. NBC News. 20/2/2017 - https://goo.gl/7PNyqG
              Twitter. @realDonaldTrump. 4/3/2017 - https://goo.gl/9Rhsuq
Lesson 8   Colin Campbell. Business Insider Australia. 19/1/2017 - https://goo.gl/ddqBSp
              Jason Linkins. Huffington Post. 24/3/2017 -

https://goo.gl/Vpx55F
Jeremy Diamond. CNN. 23/1/2016 - https://goo.gl/fozDBe
Abheet Sethi. News Bytes. 23/6/2017 -
https://goo.gl/VuniaL

Lesson 9	Editorial. Breitbart News. 27/11/2016 - https://goo.gl/MFHRjE
Lesson 10	Jason Linkins. Huffington Post. 24/3/2017 - https://goo.gl/eo3nHc
Lesson 11	Jeremy Diamond. CNN. 14/3/2017 - https://goo.gl/2r8Bsr

Chapter Three

| Lesson 12 | Grace Sparks. Huffpost. 4/1/2017 - https://goo.gl/tcSi3s |
| Lesson 13 | Jennie Matthews. Yahoo. 30/1/2017 - https://goo.gl/PV1wVh |

Kartikay Mehrotra, Erik Larson, and Bob Van Voris.
Bloomberg. 16/3/2017 - https://goo.gl/JC2TzH

| Lesson 14 | Michael Gerson. Washington Post. 27/9/2016 - https://goo.gl/Phndzb |

Marina Fang. Huffington Post. 16/3/2017 -
https://goo.gl/VZ8CUJ
Aaron Blake. Washington Post. 12/4/2017 -
https://goo.gl/1eafhi
Louis Nelson. Politico. 23/3/2017 - https://goo.gl/hxBixe

Chapter Four

| Lesson 15 | Alison Kodjak. NPR. 6/1/2017 - https://goo.gl/uShT1P |

Dave Jamieson. Huffington Post. 14/3/2017 -
https://goo.gl/Y2a3PY
Dave Jamieson. Huffington Post. 4/4/2017 -
https://goo.gl/ofCGWw
Paul Kane. The Washington Post. 15/4/2017 -
https://goo.gl/SXLJQA
Ben Westcott. CNN. 5/5/2017 - https://goo.gl/m35rk4

| Lesson 16 | Marina Fang. Huffington Post. 26/3/2017 - https://goo.gl/AS52KH |
| Lesson 17 | Sam Levine. Huffington Post. 10/3/2017 - https://goo.gl/B4bsTs |

Chapter Five

| Lesson 18 | Katie Reilly. Fortune. 24/1/2017 - https://goo.gl/tJqjNx |

Ryan Grim. Huffington Post. 24/3/2017 -
https://goo.gl/3S5TbF

| Lesson 19 | Seth Millstein. Bustle. Aug 2017 - https://goo.gl/u3VgdM |

Polly Mosendz. Bloomberg. 21/3/2017 - https://goo.gl/ZSeQ7f

Karen Yourish and Troy Griggs. The New York Times. 5/9/2017 - https://goo.gl/eadAsQ

Lesson 20   Eliza Relman. Business Insider. 17/3/2017 - https://goo.gl/RVccDu

Laura Bassett. Huffington Post. 13/4/2017 - https://goo.gl/cE8y94

Lesson 21   Dan Merica. CNN. 11/4/2017 - https://goo.gl/m9ZTDQ

Edward Helmore. The Guardian. 20/2/2017 - https://goo.gl/TdgfZh

Maya Oppenheim. Independent. 22/3/2017 - https://goo.gl/TdDNGZ

Aria Bendix. The Atlantic. 16/3/2017 - https://goo.gl/QkYsfj

Emma Brown and Devlin Barrett. Washington Post. 7/4/2017 - https://goo.gl/GTkNSu

Philip Bump. Washington Post. 8/4/2017 - https://goo.gl/3kSNNc

Willa FRej. Huffpost. 21/8/2017 - https://goo.gl/oRpzh8

Lesson 22   Eugene Robinson. Blabber Buzz. 13/4/2017 - https://goo.gl/MGDuVF

Michelle Ye Hee Lee. Washington Post. 13/4/2017 - https://goo.gl/rNU68p

David Wood. Huffington Post. 14/4/2017 - https://goo.gl/S6CBaf

Amber Phillips. The Washington Post. 14/4/2017 - https://goo.gl/nAarDr

Lesson 23   Betsy Klein. CNN. 21/1/2017 - https://goo.gl/XVwJPu

Paul Fahl. Washington Post. 10/4/2017 - https://goo.gl/fhzNAU

Gabby Morrongiello. Washington Examiner. 8/3/2016 - https://goo.gl/QJJ1YX

Carla Herreria. Huffpost. 28/6/2017 - https://goo.gl/vNrcx5

Lesson 24   Sam Levine. Huffington Post. 15/3/2017 - https://goo.gl/ZSkgCn

Jen Psaki. CNN. 22/3/2017 - https://goo.gl/peoFjb

Sam Levine. Huffington Post. 14/4/2017 - https://goo.gl/7VpFE4

Eric Bradner. CNN. 23/1/2017 - https://goo.gl/55jGWJ

Senator Ron Wyden. Huffington Post. 13/4/2017 - https://goo.gl/AKyCp8

Gregory Viscusi. Bloomberg. 27/6/2017 - https://goo.gl/7BWUhk

Ed Mazza. Huffington Post. 14/4/2017 - https://goo.gl/gJA3uW

Lesson 25	Lee Moran. Huffington Post. 21/3/2017 - https://goo.gl/MWp3tH
	Greg Sargent. Washington Post. 30/3/2017 - https://goo.gl/35b5He
	Alana Horowitz Satlin. Huffington Post. 3/4/2017 - https://goo.gl/AWFX8A
Lesson 26	Editorial Board. Washington Post. 28/3/2017 - https://goo.gl/K7XPzr
	Greg Sargent. Washington Post. 30/3/2017 - https://goo.gl/HmWX6E
	Brady Dennis and Chris Mooney. Washington Post. 9/3/2017 - https://goo.gl/tZs9mU
Lesson 27	Sokolove Law. Sokolovelaw. 2/2/2107 - https://goo.gl/vxKeT3
	Ivylise Simones. Motherjones. 9/6/2016 - https://goo.gl/5QKk66
	Staff. Mesothelioma. 28/9/2016 - https://goo.gl/QY4WrW
Lesson 28	Jennifer Ong. Morning News USA. 27/3/2107 - https://goo.gl/W2vosa
	Avi Selk. Washington Post. 15/4/2017 - https://goo.gl/eJQv23
Lesson 29	Joe Romm. Think Progress. 21/2/2017 - https://goo.gl/rF2mDg
	Editorial. MSN News. 24/3/2017 - https://goo.gl/TXpvdc
	John Wagner. MSN News. 13/6/2017 - https://goo.gl/kxQaB6
	MJ Lee. CNN. 4/5/2017 - https://goo.gl/E9H6QJ
	Dan Merica, Jim Acosta, Lauren Fox and Phil Mattingly. CNN. 14/6/2017 - https://goo.gl/Ka6VuQ
	Laura Berman Fortgang. Huffpost. 24/9/2012 - https://goo.gl/y9KPtt
Lesson 30	Sam Stein. Huffington Post. 24/3/2017 - https://goo.gl/3nkpcY
	Alan Fram. WDEL. 9/8/2017 - https://goo.gl/hb9udD
Lesson 31	Feature. The Onion. 24/1/2017 - https://goo.gl/7L7Fy1
	Isaac Arnsdorf, Josh Dawsey and Daniel Lippman. Politico. 22/12/2016 - https://goo.gl/GKAQZi
	Darryl Fears. Washington Post. 29/3/2017 - https://goo.gl/MfmQSi
	Tom Jackson. Equipment World. 12/4/2017 - https://goo.gl/yw76wH
Lesson 32	Editorial Board. Washington Post. 28/3/2017 - https://goo.gl/xVU7j5
Lesson 33	BBC. Radio NZ. 2/6/2017 - https://goo.gl/ugqY5r
	Peter Diamandis. Huffpost. 4/3/2017 -

	https://goo.gl/QfSTKy
Lesson 34	Sebastian Murdoch. Huffington Post. 25/3/2017 - https://goo.gl/7oj52q
	David Smith. The Guardian. 25/3/2017 - https://goo.gl/CQXmHW
	https://goo.gl/FBhoAz
	Abby Phillips, Jenna Johnson. The Washington Post. 6/6/2017 - https://goo.gl/tGFmHK
Lesson 35	Maxwell Strachan. Huffington Post. 10/2/2017 - https://goo.gl/LxB2N5
	James Rothwell and Barney Henderson. The Telegraph. 17/3/2017 - https://goo.gl/BjH4fz
	Chris Cillizza. CNN. 29/5/2017 - https://goo.gl/Q9E2yS

Chapter 6

Lesson 36	Drew Harwell. Independent. 16/12/2016 - https://goo.gl/ppCYAA
Lesson 37	Drew Harwell, Anu Narayanswamy. The Washington Post. 20/11/2016 - https://goo.gl/LUBtrD

Chapter 7

Lesson 38	Rachael Bade, Josh Dawsey, Jennifer Haberkorn. Politico. 23/3/2017 - https://goo.gl/6W6CNZ
Lesson 39	Amber Jamieson. The Guardian. 9/3/210 - https://goo.gl/opBQtv
	Definition of transformational leadership Wikipedia Source - https://goo.gl/qSGGrf
Lesson 40	Zach Toombs. Newsy. 10/5/2017 - https://goo.gl/315ncs
	Lisa Rein, Abby Phillip. The Washington Post. 17/6/2017 - https://goo.gl/cTrAeJ
Lesson 41	Reuters. Politics. 25/3/2017 - https://goo.gl/MCFuLt
	Lauren Fox, MJ Lee. CNN. 15/3/2017 - https://goo.gl/BhSjvn
	Janet Shan. Hinterland Gazette. 4/5/2017 - https://goo.gl/CB8mvs
Lesson 42	Matthew Lee, Josh Lederman. Yahoo. 13/6/2017 - https://goo.gl/KGJ4Jn
Lesson 43	Gerard Tubb. Sky News. 22/3/2017 - https://goo.gl/ux1Brn
Lesson 44	Ashley Parker and Philip Rucker. Washington Post.. 26/3/2017 - https://goo.gl/M1h997
Lesson 45	Jason Linkins. Huffington Post. 27/3/2017 - https://goo.gl/PTKkbQ

Chapter 8

Lesson 46	Ruth Ben-Ghiat. CNN. 1/2/2017 - https://goo.gl/j5Eo5C
	Conor Friedersdorf. The Atlantic. 25/8/2016 -

https://goo.gl/HmC6S4
Lesson 47   Maxwell Tani. Business Insider. 12/12/2016 -
https://goo.gl/GE1SSY
Lesson 48   Zach Carter, Ben Walsh, Christina Wilkie. Huffington Post.
7/4/2017 - https://goo.gl/8UkScc
Josh Rogin. Bloomberg. 15/3/2016 - https://goo.gl/N3bmZX
Jacob Pramuk. CNBC. 19/5/2017 - https://goo.gl/Y1TyNs
Jim Acosta. CNN. 12/5/2017 - https://goo.gl/BU916F
Jeff Mason, Patricia Zengerle. Reuters. 16/5/2017 -
https://goo.gl/TGAZJb
Pauline Gross. Giz Press. 24/6/2017 - https://goo.gl/xSEB3J
Bloomberg News. SCMP. 22/6/2017 - https://goo.gl/JccMPP

Chapter 9

Lesson 49   Michael Hudson. Counterpunch. 28/11/2017 -
https://goo.gl/5BhKrR
Zach Carter, Arthur Delaney. Huffington Post. 16/3/2017 -
https://goo.gl/gNJSYN
Jenna Johnson. Washington Post. 2/4/2017 -
https://goo.gl/TgF89a
Michael Hudson, Sharmini Peries. Counterpunch.
28/11/2017 - https://goo.gl/Er5N7Q
Edward Wong. The Star. 29/3/2017 - https://goo.gl/ncv5EU

Chapter 11

I   Abby Phillip. Washington Post. 26/8/2017 -
https://goo.gl/xye2uc
Editorial. American Bridge 21st Century. 24/4/2017 -
https://goo.gl/qvGo2Y
Jeremy Diamond. CNN. 27/7/2017 - https://goo.gl/A7V6KH
Megan Cassidy. USA Today. 25/8/2017 -
https://goo.gl/fU8cTp
II   Claire Toueille. International Business Times. 25/8/2017 -
https://goo.gl/yc7kae
IV   Chris Kenning and Joseph Ax. Huffpost. 7/8/2017 -
https://goo.gl/S8KEoi
Paige Lavender. Huffpost. 4/8/2017 -
https://goo.gl/mgZ4gD
Michael R. Strain. Bloomberg. 16/8/2017 -
https://goo.gl/MouJdR
Armin Rosen. Tablet Mag. 1/4/2017 - https://goo.gl/Tz8rbs
Steve Eder and Dave Philipps. The New York Times.
1/8/2016 - https://goo.gl/ZF1yTi
Sara Jayne. Left Voice. 20/8/2017 - https://goo.gl/xBbL6H

NOTE: Please note that long form URL links to reference material in the Bibliography have been converted into short URL links in the interest of conserving space.

Image Credits

Cover
Design by Don Henderson

Lesson 13
Photo by Vlad Tchompalov - Source: Unsplash

Lesson 29
Lincoln Memorial at Night. Photo by Aaron Murphy - Source: Freeimage

Lesson 32
Chinese Polution. Photo by Nadya Pamuk - Source: Freeimage
Bleached Coral. Photo by Oregon State University - Source: Wikimedia Commons
Hurricane Harvey. Photo by NASA Goddard Space Flight Center from Greenbelt, MD, USA   [CC BY 2.0], via Wikimedia Commons
Hurricane Irma. Photo by Ministry of Defense, Netherlands [CC0], via Wikimedia Commons

Lesson 43
Ivanka Trump. Photo by US Department of State (Public Domain) - Source: Wikimedia Commons

Lesson 44
Jared Kushner. By Chairman of the Joint Chiefs of Staff from Washington D.C, United States (Public Domain) - Source: Wikimedia

Lesson 46
Steve Bannon. By Gage Skidmore from Peoria, AZ, United States of America [CC BY- SA 2.0] - Source: Wikimedia Commons

Lesson 48
Vladimir Putin. By kremlin.ru [CC BY 4.0], via Wikimedia Commons - Source: Wikimedia Commons

www.ingramcontent.com/pod-product-compliance
Lightning Source LLC
Chambersburg PA
CBHW071552200326
41519CB00021BB/6716